Poems for
Praise
Comfort
And Joy
Volume 3

RONALD JIROVEC

Poems for
Praise
Comfort
And Joy
Volume 3

RONALD JIROVEC

Kravitz & Sons
INNOVATORS IN PUBLISHING, MARKETING AND ADVERTISING

Kravitz and Sons LLC
1301 Farmville Blvd, Suite 104
Greenville, NC 27834

Published by Kravitz and Sons LLC.

ISBN: 979-8-89639-249-1 (sc)
ISBN: 979-8-89639-250-7 (e)

Library of Congress Control Number: 2025907853

Table of Contents

Author's Foreword

I feel that my writing shall be an adventurous lifetime odyssey. I describe this in "My Odyssey." I pen my knowledge and experience in rhyming lines, with some interesting variations to some of them. I know and write the truth of the Word. Such truth must be guarded and protected.

At present I think the ultimate a writer can do is ascent to the great intellectual prowess of John Milton and at times exhibit the style of Nahum in lyric poetry of a high order and exude his emotion. He is considered to be the most impassioned of all the prophets.

Come with me now to step into a world of knowledge; go beyond wisdom with insight; explore a few moments of the afterlife as the redeemed see their Savior face-to-face and the lost step into a cold, confusing darkness; discover the moment and place you first get to behold the beautiful Holy Spirit's face and person. See how I describe going back to the future, wrestle with some great philosophical questions, be challenged with some intellectual conjecture, and go trekking in the high country.

Chapter five contains meditations on 50 foreign phrases. See how these adages have a practical application to us today.

Use of similes, metaphors, and interesting quips continue. One in this book is about spiritual gifts. "If you are not using your spiritual gift, it is no better than a bottle out on a sea adrift."

Good reading to you.

Looking Down from the High Sierra
February 1, 1991

From the vantage so high
I could look far out and down as well as nigh.
The view from Glacier Point
was not one to disappoint.
For adequate words most would be at a loss.
My eyes swept from the valley floor to Half Dome across.
The 16-mile trek
did and shall again beck.
The general path my eyes surveyed.
Adventure the hike fully purveyed.
The full hike makes for an arduous day.
Now easily my eyes can just now sweep the full way.
People trekked it from times of old.
The adventurous had much magnificence to behold.
Too many did stop
only one tenth of the way to the top.
I have not yet attained Half Dome's peak.
For what high goal do you seek?

I see the one way climb as life's path
full of strain, pleasure, joy and sometimes wrath.
As we will all one day stand before God
we will quickly view the path we trod.
It will occur of a verity and not per chance.
Life shall go by our eyes like the path's quick glance.
What is your spiritual goal?
God must help you define it so your trek be spiritually full.
The path and rewards are quite unknown to full attainment.
The short hikers shall surely not experience spiritual fulfillment.
Evil wishes you to think a high journey is too tough.
Many will stop when things first get rough.
Unknown rewards shall be found
for every step to higher ground.
Pity that for a little pain
too many as "lowlanders" shall remain.
By faith step forward and out.
There will be times of fear and doubt.
Many who get to the higher plateaus
may rue they lingered so long in their comfy chateaus.

To stop or slow you evil will lure and entice.
They want you to think your lowland meadow is quite nice.
They will set a trap with a worldly vice.
To keep you from going forth it is a good device.
By cunning, guile, whims, and shame they will try
to keep you from the high, blue, magnificent sky.

From heaven all will be put into proper perspective.
Now is the time to consider what is ahead and be reflective.
Reflect upon the past and what could be ahead.
Will judgment yield many rewards or will you dread?
You will see how close you came to life's highest possible view
or if you too soon stopped and went askew.
To know what is all ahead I know not.
Evil would like me to sit and wish I would rot.
Pray God takes you to your Half Dome's crown.
Anything less is something to lament over and frown.
I saw down to the path as portraying human life.
For spiritual examples it was very rife.
To look down from heaven's terra firma
may be like looking down from the High Sierra.

Headin' up the San Luis Obispo Way
February 4, 1992

From the Santa Barbara beach to Yosemite Valley.
Later we went to the high country.
Our several trips went quite well.
The valley was up the road quite a spell.
A rather nice trip I should say.
It took the better part of a day.
A stop was in line after a while I would agree.
My friend (D W) absolutely needed a cup of coffee.
He had this as a favorite spot along the line.
I thought it would also be quite fine.
Up the coastal highway and here a turn.
We headed more inland I did learn.

We probably went by the place twice
and went into town on the thrice.
More time to visit I need to give.
It seemed like a nice place to live.
A nice community
they would probably quite well agree.
It strikes a good remembrance.

More visits could a fondness enhance.
Fork to the left back to the sea.
To the right inland and rolling hills to see.

One must not labor only to pile up treasure.
God's creation is for our pleasure.
A creation from times of old.
So much beauty to behold.
On to Paso Robles to bear right.
On to the high country to enjoy many a sight.
Many other parks and places to go.
Much, much to see and know.
Nigh on to two years and I need to get back.
How I yearn again trekking up a mountain track.
Nostalgia yearns to plan ahead to the day
my friend and I can be headin' up the San Luis Obispo way!

Trekking in the High Country.
August 30, 1992

Consider now your own spiritual state.
Does it produce within a favorable debate?
Hopefully you can see some progression
and not at all a condition of stagnation.
If each day you have a prayerful talk,
you should also see something of a spiritual walk.
Consider that some Christians after forty years
are yet in a state that should cause some tears.
Somehow you got stuck in the bog
and too many concepts never got out of the fog.
You who go a little get to the beautiful green valley.
Though beautiful it is not here you want to ever dally.
There is much in the high meadows and mountains to see.
Beautiful flowers, peaks, mesas, and springs of a different degree.
Ask the Lord to show you your hindering chains.
The high country is a wow and has many gains.
Pity your climb should fail.
Ask God to get you on the right trail.
Too many will indeed later greatly cry
because they did not even really try.
The climb is not one you figure out alone.
The same Christ works in you who sits on the throne.
Many shall perish from a state of harlotry and whoredom.
You will only be one step up in your stagnation and boredom.
The dragon has come to destroy, distort, and cheat.

To rob you of spiritual rewards is for him a successful feat.
Ponder again if your heading or climb makes you sad
or if "Christ is working in me" and for that I am glad.
Examine your state not for any type of bragger,
but merely to know if you are trekking in the high country.

Half Dome – An Inevitable Return
January 24, 1993

Who can fully describe all of the park's lure
or majestic grandeur?
Each trip had a role
in inspiring me to pen a new goal.
On the last trip Half Dome was attained. *
It gave consideration for what remained.

It shall never become a dull story
to describe the Creator's handiwork and glory.
There are many more places to see.
More magnificence to behold you should agree.
Certain things one has to do rightly.
In much we therefore must think reflectively.
In a few things it matters much
that a project gets the proper finishing touch.
No less than one hike to Half Dome the situation does demand.
Last time I went with no camera in hand.
It was to our fate the morn was getting late.
Camera without we went in haste
as we had no time to waste.
I remembered once when we got one mile on track.
We had no time to go back.
Someone took two pictures of us that day.
They never came our way.

Of the Creator's high country, I shall never get tired.
There is more (than I have time) to be admired.
Only to see and wonder does my trip require.
To write it is God that does additionally inspire.
The idea of a return conquest does not cease or stop.
I have to get picture of myself at the top.
Perhaps some things in life are just an inadequate mime.
Ask the Lord to make them more meaningful in time.
Perhaps of McArthur's 3 famous words you did learn. **
I must likewise describe Half Dome as an inevitable return.

*I and my hiking companion, Danny Walters, made the tip
of Half Dome around July 1992. Thank you, Danny, for joining me
on this arduous 14-mile hike with a 1,000-foot elevation gain.
We made the hike from 12 noon to 7 p.m. We had to get to the base
of the mountain before 7 p.m. to catch the last bus back to camp Curry.
Missing it would have 1 mile mile to our hike. After 14 miles, no thanks!

** "I shall return"

A Proud Heritage

March 26, 1991

For the raising of many children, what is one's wage?
Soon all reach the later years and reflective stage.
All will consider whether their children are lost in the crowd
or they are the cause to be proud.
Much and unknown shall be the reward
of those who influence their children to serve the Lord.
Proud indeed if many be missionaries in the field,
but to other purposes of God we must also yield.
There is not just one type of work God extols.
Hath not the body and workers many roles?
It is good to be a missionary to a foreign land,
but can everyone be a hand?
The mission must have its home-base insiders
and there must yet be providers.
All who do the will of God will He elevate.
John Milton said they also serve God who stand and wait.

But to a few others I must say
that your teaching does not guarantee a spiritual way.
"Train up a child and when he is older," the scripture does say
that he will not depart from this way.
The Proverbs are given as principles you need note.
Some quote this proverb in a manner as rote.
God does not promise man shall not thereafter sin.
Some children will still greatly error and their parents will chagrin.
As parents you can only do your best,
then all results and consequences in the hand of God must rest.

But it is really great that you can tell
everyone that with your many children all goes well.
Influence well the path your children need trod
and then you will have to accept the will and sovereignty of God.
Praise and rejoice in the Lord if all goes as says the Proverbs sage.
Such a resultant shall indeed bring a proud heritage.

Just Wondering

December 4, 1996

First went abroad when she was very small.
Fifteen years later back home and now quite tall.
Parents serving the Lord across the sea.
Where the Lord wanted them, they did agree.
She and the sibs grew up in a faraway place.
There and Santa Barbara running a very different race.
A very foreign land to grow up together.
All very different the people, customs, and the weather.
Learning morals, values, and very much.
How different this land now after the plane did retouch.

Now after high school a very different course.
Getting to apply every mental resource.
So many new things to learn
and learning how to just discern.
Thinking, reflecting about the people behind.
Now here a new life to course and find.
A college and plan to go four years ahead.
On this course she thought she was led.
A direct plan and course which to proceed.
Thence from there to a career this would lead.

But after only one year she felt the need to depart.
Strange turn and a good plan to fall apart?
The course did greatly veer.
For what purpose did this now appear?
Obediently she had to depart.
I quite sense at the first college remained a bit of her heart.
Interruption of this plan for years of four.
About the Lord she is surely now learning more.
God knows it all and the end in His planning.
Perhaps quite often as a typical person she is left "just wondering."

(This m.k. returned to California after 1-2 year break and
went back to her college.)

One Went Home
(An Elegy for Cassie Bernall)

April 25 & 28, 1999

I   Oh, world full of sin.

You give much too much to which we chagrin.
We indeed live in an evil tumultuous age.
How oft we see the fires of wickedness rage.
So suddenly at times erupts a tragic plight.
Not exempt form the tragedies are the children of the Light.

Sin will from the face of the earth every life erase.
How beautiful to see our Savior face to face.
Oh, children of the King you shall then no longer rove and roam.
The Lord Jesus will take us home.

II   How many will stand up for the Lord we need ask.
At times know that this will be a difficult task.
Not often need the most falter and doubt.
The spiritual enemy wants to take us out.
"Will you stand up for me?" asks the King.
At times only the brave dare do such a thing.

Tragedy and wickedness will at times our lives erase.
How beautiful to see the Savior face to face.
Oh, children of the King you need no longer roam.
The Lord Jesus will take us home.

III One brave girl for her Lord did stand
The lives of the saints were in evil demand.
Of the sixteen she was perhaps the only one.
My dear, for you this day the martyr's reward was won.
Family saddened, but she did rejoice to see her Lord.
Father and Holy Spirit show her now her great reward.

Family indeed saddened by the life tragedy did erase.
Indescribably beautiful to see her Savior face to face.
Your time came and you need no longer roam.
In this I rejoice to know that one went home.

IV   She was only here for a short while.
Why – she was just learning life's style.
Everyone has their appointed time to abide.
Tis not for us to know the why or when He takes us aside.
Your departure was indeed sad.
But over your manifest destiny we rejoice and are glad.

You ended well your worldly race.
You stood for Him and moments later with Him face to face.
In this world you now would not want to roam.
Joyously exalted in that heaven is your new home.

V   Up through the stars you went.
     The Father's appointed time so the Savior was sent.
     Through the Valley of the Shadow of Death His hold was tight.
     Twas not long before you saw heaven's light.
     The Holy Spirit should have been the first to welcome her.
     He did indwell you and was omnipresent too you should concur.

In time all bad memories will the Lord erase.
We will remember only being with the Lord face to face.
Now in heaven she can joyously roam.
The triune God is everywhere in your new home.

Another Prayer for Christina
January 31, 2015

Some ducks, a bottle, and a few other items at which one may look.
To top them all 3 poems (now 4) in a book.
Years of acquaintance close to seven.
The first meeting indeed planned by the God of heaven.
Now as I look back
she had an event filled track.
Her church dad's life was one of routine, not too adventurous, and one of stability.
She had to dodge disasters and avoid tragedies with utmost agility.
So long she has to fight the evil force.
Life oft seemed to be just a mental obstacle course.
Once a week she would see her "church dad."
Some bucks, a hug, and for a smile she became glad.
At the end of the dark tunnel he was her light.
The once a week visit with his tacos and extra bacon was a delight.

Plagued for a while by a jealous hacker.
Finally, a judge became a corrective smacker.
O Lord for her woes and disappointing tears
give her now much relief and blessed years.
Let your spirit guide her on her way.
Give her a lofty spirit to help her trek along each day.
Bestow upon her wisdom and discretion.
Lord, You are her means and provision.
Give her wisdom and insight for every decision.
May she now be able to merrily roll along
and within her "bubble up a tune" for a joyous song.
(Christian, do you need to be dad, mom, uncle, aunt etc.
for someone in your church?)

Woe the Judgment Hand
March 30, 1991

From one point, be not rocked.
God is not mocked.
What we sow, we shall reap.
It matters a heap.
For all sin we must pay.
Holiness is God's way.

Judgment is manifested in many ways.
These are seen by the observance of days.
Loss of heavenly rewards is a cost.
Monetary or worldly goods can be "lost."
Our body with disease or malady God may inflict.
Our children could be struck down or undergo undue conflict.
A consequence for sin will be unfailing.
"You are o.k. Nothing is happening," is evil lying and misleading.

As soon as God sees your sin occurring,
He gives some type of warning.
He is patient and long-suffering.
Stern wrath is seldom immediately impending.
Perhaps He may send a fellow saint to warn.
So, catch your sinful act while it is yet early morn.
All deeds have consequences.
There is a great variation in the "subsequences."
With your sin God is dealing
will be the later revealing.
Flee the sin lest you become enslaved.
After too long you will be greatly depraved.
If for the state of your sin you are getting a warning,
confess it quickly so there be only a slight chastening.
Eventually a severe judgment upon you shall land.
Woe then the judgment hand.
For one my mind saw the judgement hand ready to go out.
It was the judgement hand I knew without a doubt.
So sinning saint, take heed before it is too late.
Woe betide your terrible fate.

To Where from the Slingshot?
August 16, 1991

Around and around the world goes.
When man gets off – only God knows.
Around and around David's slingshot went.
At the predetermined time the stone was sent.
Once gone – right on track.
Never to come back!

The world spinning in space.
Man upon it soaring somewhere as in a race.
The earth whirring around the sun.
To some place this solar system is flung.
At the divine slinger many do scoff.
Oh fool – you will also be a stone to be flung off!

David's stones had great impact.
Man and stone's great consequence – a sure fact.
Goliath surely fell.
For your ten count shall a bell surely knell.
The body one day at rest.
Its spirit and soul it shall surely divest.
To heaven or hell – opt your spot!
To where from the slingshot?

Beyond Intellectual Assent
November 2, 1991

Tis a simple fact of "salvation by the cross."
Scripture warns that the majority will be "at loss."
Perhaps too many think if they say, "Yea, yea Lord,"
they shall have their eternal reward.
Eternal life shall not be thrust to you on a silver platter,
so, contemplate the fact as it does greatly matter.
For many the assurance of eternal life is a nebulous blur.
You need to be surer of what shall occur.
Though in Jesus you believe,
eternal life one does not automatically receive.
To also receive, accept and trust
is a must.
Salvation Christ will impart
if your head knowledge goes deep into your heart.
On obtaining eternal life you must be bent.

Know that it goes beyond intellectual assent.

Then contemplate walking on a higher spiritual plane.
Too many in the lowland do remain.
One's knowledge needs to have breadth
and one's spiritual insight must have depth.
You have heard, 'He (or she) is very shallow.
One can't reap from ground lying fallow.
The enigma is surely one that does confound
many as man himself can't till spiritual ground.
Can man himself ascend to God on high?
My mind augments little this occlusive objective when I try.
Know also it depends upon God's will.
You can only be willing
and pray that God does the filling.
"God, transform this undesirous heart.
Make me a fitful vessel that Thy virtue can impart.
In time I may be fit
to bear fruit of the spirit.
Thus, at thy feet my request does lie.
Only You know the outcome of beyond and nigh."
Spiritual depth has its aspect of unfathomable mysteriousness.
Attempts by man to logic his way could be deliriousness.
On obtaining spiritual depth you must be prayerfully bent.
Know that it goes beyond intellectual assent.

Destiny's Apocalypse
December 1, 1991

If it be bad, it will be bad, if good, then hurrah.
Some simply think que sera, sera.
It is simple to say fate and forces
will run their courses.
This explanation is seemingly simplistic,
but not at all realistic.
Importance of your life does command
that you learn of the Creator and all forces at hand.
You know much will be accomplished by work, choice,
and a persuasive voice.
A certain something you want that you see.
You can make this to be.
For as long as your life does abide,
evil forces will be by your side.
I say there is better way to see
what will be.

The woman or man
covered by the blood has in store a divine plan.
The rest need also contemplate
what shall be their possible fate.
The obedient to God shall find
that the unfolding of His plan shall come to their mind.
You disobedient tarry in foolish hesitation.
God would rather you partake of His wonderful revelation.
God is in command.
He controls all forces at hand.
Life will have more purpose and less mystery.
God wishes to reveal your wonderful, manifest destiny.
The forces causing you much woe
will someday go.
They will abide until your last breath.
Heaven will be a great victory upon your death.
You spirit seeing a myriad of angels will be a surprise.
It is written that the tempter and his force will meet their demise.
You in the Word and the light shall see much eclipse.
We redeemed will be on hand to see destiny's apocalypse.

Two Departed
February 23, 1991

Two souls snatched from their ways.
Surely a vast number by such put in a daze.
No doubt it was not their time.
We who survey knew they were not in their prime.
Two in the same high school class.
A month and an obit for twice a lass.
"She had a zest for life."
Perhaps two not over encumbered by strife.
Sobering to those yet running life's race.
Lightning does not strike twice in the same place
I thought as a general rule.
Alas, it did in their school.

Ye who remain take note.
You may not rest in what someone wrote.
Perhaps each was lauded as good.
Heaven bounded they surely should.
But, O Death you again played your role
and we need think upon your toll.
Sooner or later we shall meet.
The odds may no one beat.

The Creator of every spark and flame
said, "It is time," and death came.
You two need be heavy on every mind.
Was it eternal light or darkness you did find?
"Christ died for our sins," it was said.
If you think all are heaven bound, you have mistakenly read.
Now for eternity you are sealed.
To you destiny was revealed.
The gift of life through Christ you needed to take.
Confession and acceptance, you could not forsake.
I hope you held Christ personally dear,
but, I fear.

Blind Bartimaeus
March 15, 1992

From town to town did Jesus often go.
One day He was on the road to Jericho.
The blind Bartimaeus,
son of Timaeus,
sat by the road begging.
When he heard that Jesus was coming
he cried, "Thou son of David, have mercy on me.
Someone said, "Be of good comfort. He calleth thee."
To Jesus he went.
Jesus did not ask that he repent.
"What will thou that I do unto thee?"
"Lord, that I might see."
Jesus told him to go his way
as his faith made him whole that day.
Immediately he received his sight
and followed Jesus with great delight.

Consider the blind man who was made to see.
His faith and wisdom were greater than others to a great degree.
No miracles he saw.
Those who could see had some thinking with a great flaw.
You Pharisees were surely deceived.
His works you saw, but Jesus was not at all well received.
You who have eyes to see.
Behold the works of the Creator Christ of an infinite degree.
Read, see, behold, and understand what is before your eyes.
Stepping into eternity need not be a surprise.
Your eyes should enhance your judgment
now or you will surely later greatly lament.

Bartimaeus is a good example of one by the wayside
who just believed and ever thereafter with Christ shall abide.
Many with full senses do greatly lack
in that they will blindly go down the wrong eternal track.
Bartimaeus is a good example of a blind man being right
and far exceeding the majority with their sight.

The Mind's Advance
June 30, 1991

A few things of sound and sense
come now to my defense!
Men of old in poetry did reflect.
Much wisdom – a coveted object.
Words so learned, intense, and from wisdom so deep.
Come hence my guard to keep.
Many were so intellectually high.
A trite (and vain??) stab at understanding I try.
Some of Solomon's discernment I ask.
Comprehension of some – an impossible task.
A prayer to heaven's shore.
Understanding I implore!
Their wisdom with the Word,
let it in my mind's understanding be heard.
Many tools and tokens of wisdom to grasp.
A near impossible task.
Give my mind's eye greater height.
Yea, it can by Thy might.
Sharpen my mind to quickly draw and reflect.
Impede my foe – wisdom's rays he would deflect.
Power at my left
wills my sanity and understanding be bereft.
Centuries of wisdom to read.
More understanding I prayerfully plead!
Pope and Milton of the Lord well I knew.
In the highness of a mighty mind they soared and flew.
The Lord's helper was by your side.
From them higher wisdom came and did abide.
Over so much to pore.
Centuries of writing, poetry, lore, and more.
My wisdom and ability I wish to advance.
From source divine it will not be chance.
Almost galaxies of wisdom and knowledge to traverse.
Alexander and John – we shall one day converse.
Volumes of poetry before me in which to bask.
Where to start? Such a task!
Thus, for the remainder of years lying ahead,
Let me course much knowledge and be thus well mindfully fed.

Whence and Whereby my Soul
December 28, 1991

Let us contemplate not to be confusing,
but to put forth thoughts in a philosophical and percipient musing.
Why of all the places in the world
was my soul in this particular place and frame be hurled?
Predictable genetics bringing a body to a particular plot.
An instantly created spark and flame* by divine lot.
Man's understanding of this making limited progress.
Grasping the creator's high plan – no chance of success.
Thus, one must channel his musing
or he will enter madness and the state not just confusing.
Or can there be a wise man named
who can explain how the universe was framed?
Certainly, you will have no strife
as you are also in control of your eternal life!
Some like-minded gods had a wild concoction in their head
as their madness ceased and they went to the dead.
Thus, wild raver you played the fool
as you must have been governed by a higher rule.
To others of like madness, you exacted a good ploy,
but to higher beings you were being pawned as a dumb toy.

To this place my soul was chosen.
Billions of other times and places it could have fallen.
Thus, if you think you have a miserable state,
know there is always a place of more unfortunate fate.
Understanding purpose is knowing your role.
A few finding none snuffed their flame and the bells toll.
A few brilliant poets by reading I knew.
Empty brilliance and they sadly, eternally went askew.
Over the cuckoo's nest a few of us think we flew
as a vision and the goal from insight nary grew.
Most seem to traverse an ordinary course,
but mine comes from the mysterious part of the divine source.
Things quite unconventional and strange intervenings on the track.
How often we would have recourse if we could go back.
The power whereby my soul is also the exacter of whereto.
How long we yearned destiny's turning point too.
Thus, we hope·to soon escape our seemingly mundane plight.
Let our course to residence number seven take flight.
Yea, we know our present number six
was to be a rather temporary fix.
Now more understandable is the whence and whereby.
The whereto is the impossible enigma for which our understanding does cry.
The high whereby

is the key to why.
Conjecture just takes me around and around.
Oh Lord, we hope the hidden portal entrance will soon be found.
* An illusion to "Vital Spark of Heavenly Flame" by Alexander Pope.

A Curse? The Dross? A Perplexity!
March 20, 1992

For what great sin
did the curse begin?
For those who hate the Lord will He visit the transgressions
of the fathers unto the third and fourth generations.
This is not just an old wives' tale with a flaw.
Moses wrote it four times in the book of the law.
To see something written more than twice
means it is being stressed should by any scholar's advice.
For those who repent the Lord will show great mercy,
but will by no means clear the guilty.
Over the later generations most would lament.
Thus, goes the declared judgment.
The idea of a curse many would resist,
but scripture does appear to insist.

Defining a curse becomes a complexity
and a perplexity.
Human judgment can't easily say so and so
must be a curse as things do seem to go.
The curse would go beyond mere bad luck or chance.
It is not just a single misstep in life's dance.
A couple of generations one must study
to see if they appear ill-fated from previous iniquity.
Perhaps consecutive generations of early widowhood
would fit with the wife left to raise a small or large brood.
Surely a man with many children and no wife
would be in for a lot of strife.
The idea of the same thing happening after and before
would be a "luck situation" most would deplore.
Having children with much ill-luck or ill-health
and accidents keeping one from accumulating any wealth
seem to strengthen the case.
Quite a few facts as of such give the "curse theory" a base.
Consider if the offspring be children of the Lord,
and they are getting a two-sided "reward."
For the original sin is the going forth of the sword,
but consider all who suffer like Job will gain a good reward.

Thus, the general path
seems predetermined by wrath.
God also loves his redeemed children.
Also, of their spiritual growth and nurture we can pen.

Each redeemed child is to have growth and sanctification.
God does not create souls merely to vent indignation.
Thus, in the new testament it is told
that the dross comes forth from the refining of the gold.
Know that each really took the fire and the heat.
To say tribulation is for sin or purification you can only try.
Far above us is God's "why."
In deliberate sin one can be quite secretive and devious.
The sin of others is quite obvious.
For sinful ways punishment will be in demand.
Know that some loss or punishment will be at hand.
Dare not say immediately that suffering is for sin.
Know that it may be that sanctification did begin.
So, some children inherit an iniquitous estate.
Redeemed by the blood takes them to a final higher state.
Many children simply continue in the great sin
that their forefathers did begin.
We need also then take pity that the children of disobedience
will have a sad inheritance.
Some of the future generations will be redeemed and some will not.
It is God's predestination that will determine their lot.

Surely some of this is like a door that does revolve.
After going around and around the perplexity comes to no resolve.
Some theories seem obvious and are quite plain.
Lost in God's mysteriousness shall many things remain.
By trying to picture a labyrinth some will be amused.
In pondering greatly, others will become even more confused.
For mysteriousness and complex pondering many of us thirst.
Others may later become more confused than their state of the first.
Meditation of God's mysteriousness causes us to go intellectually higher
and simultaneously seems like we are now even a bit madder.
From the lowland you heard that the truth will make you free.
There is different trekking in the high country.
We are not talking of simple gravitational rules.
Expounding mysteriousness can turn the wisest into fools.
So, jump into such a high-minded debate, if you dare.
Look to God and you may be surprised at how you fare.
From experience I tell you that meditation of God's Word
shall indeed lend a rich reward.
Step up to a higher plane and enter a new realm.
Some things can surely overwhelm.

Your previously learned rules of one and one makes two
will no longer adequately well do.
Many facets of the spiritual world form a complexity.
Such as "A Curse? The Dross? A Perplexity!"
(The curse declared: Exodus 20:5, 34:7, Numbers 14:18, Deut. 5:9)

Glass Stones and Spectrums
June 21, 1992

Imagine a pile of various shaped glass stones.
Piled in a corner they are no better than old bones.
Such idleness was not the maker's design.
Not to be useless concoctions either the sine or cosine.
Not even you evolutionists should be fooled
in that all shapes beyond ore were tooled.
Surely many things go the way of the plight
if not utilized in the proper light.
Take the multi-surfaced stones out of the dust and night.
Shine them up and put them into the full sunlight.
Now a beautiful multi-colored spectrum to behold.
A different story of such can now be told.
For such stones neglect was an abuse.
Oh, how different when put to its designed use.

Every Christian is the Lord's gem.
Self-conceived purpose is just a stratagem.
Without God you will remain a dusty, dark stone.
Too many are as such and are not alone.
Your life will more resemble a plight.
You need an infusion of divine light.
You and others can be quite surprised.
The outpouring is of beauty and wonder comprised.
Ponder the stone and the sun.
Likewise, is the Christian and the Son.
We are the branch and Christ the vine.
The coming forth of fruit and gems from a rich mine.
God is all of the power and light.
He who effuses the Holy Spirit forth is like a wonderful sight.
Without God people will be just conundrums and humdrums.
So much better to be shining glass stones and spectrums.

Perspective of your Goings
July 1, 1992

Consider your many comings
and goings.
Is your perception of a few things in a fog?
Does life feel like you are always doing a tiring jog?
Are you satisfied in your present state?
All have problems, we need not debate.
Does your present job or work seem well life's goal?
Examine your spiritual role.
One's own meditation usually falls quite short.
You may likely come up with an inadequate report.
Man's own way shall ever be a plight.
You need to ask Christ for divine introspective light.
Your devotional time is necessary
and can be quite enlightening as well as revolutionary.
Upon your knees great things can begin.
It is more that a time to give thanks and confess sin.
Some may be shocked when they see the mirror of reality.
Others can be enlightened to divine opportunity.
Some of you are going into a less satisfying state.
You may be confronting a move, not a forever fate.
Get in tune with God and you may learn
you are about to take a turn.
An unfulfilled spiritual life you are not to ever spend.
God wishes all to have an expected end.
To the Lord's law and Word, you must be obedient.
Only then will your life be more spiritually excellent.
Surely many need to come out of the spiritual darkness.
Do you wonder why life does continually regress?
Ye, who seek the Lord
shall have the best reward.
The multitude of the world exhibits "self-destroyings."
Jesus can give an amazing enlightenment to the perspective of your goings.

On Philosophical Introspection
July 5, 1992

Many philosophers have done an introspection.
Too many fell short with a limited self-reflection.
Too much, "I think; therefore, I am," rumination
and not enough "Why am I?" retrospection.
Is not Satan and the power of his angels quite overt?

Surely then you should believe also in the more covert.
The working of Satan is quite manifest.
We Christians perceive quite well the rest.
Mixing God with philosophy is a concept many would jeer.
How much more complete are those who think God is one to revere!
Every philosopher must see the sheer pointlessness of living
in a Godless world or you are very unexacting.
You have not come to a correct "I am"
and statement of purpose is incorrect and a sham.
God has said, "My works declare me."
Pity for you if you do not agree.
Unless you agree to the above point one,
no good philosophical introspection has begun.

Point two is you should believe God has a plan
for his creation called man.
I speak of those who have found redemption.
We are only saved by the shed blood and there is no exception.
Read much about servanthood.
Read and ponder much about a Christly brotherhood.
Jesus came as a servant too.
He has a like mannered role for me and you.
Life is more than go to church, live,
do our work, and faithfully give.
Servanthood requires an enhancement via reflection.
One becomes more enhanced by a resolute introspection.
We have spiritual gifts to fit into the body.
It is a point each needs to study.
The redeemed of heaven and earth are Christ's body macrocosm.
Each local church is a microcosm.
We are the clay on the potter's wheel.
We are each made an important part you should feel.
"Study to show thyself approved."
The body is hurt when a part is inactive or removed.
Meditation can lead to important discoveries.
We can gain peace and remove anxieties.
The focal body is perceived better by God's enlightenment.
We have limited ability by pure empirical judgment.
The Christian can indeed go above and beyond
the natural man fishing from his scholastic pond.
With God's help you can perceive your role with insight
and come about a much greater delight.
Let God magnify the perception of your role
and your introspection has become wonderfully more whole.

God does not create clones with His power.
Every person is uniquely designed to individually flower.

On philosophical introspection I see
point number three
as discovering your unique personalities.
Indeed, we are not machine stamp-outs like from factories.
Part of this is by God's revelation.
He enhances or hinders by divine magnification.
By obedience one's talents can come to full bloom.
Man alone might otherwise just as well look for a speck in a big ballroom.
If upon a disobedient course one does embark,
one's blessings shall remain hidden in the dark.
God does thereby decide if one's exertions are to be full
and successful or should be a null.
With God's help your unusual, hidden abilities can flourish.
Your church work and fulfillment will be a thing to greater cherish.
One's life and introspection by Christ's hand take flight
and thus, in seeing ourselves for God's purpose has great delight.

On Unique Peculiarities
July 17, 1992

If you have upon several thousand different snowflakes made a note,
you will know that God does not like repetitive rote.
Nonconformity to singleness is God's originality.
Yea, even people are created with variety and individuality.
The eternal spark and flame are non-human entities.
The Creator puts together all personalities.
Sanguine, choleric,
melancholy, phlegmatic.
Mostly one or a blend of several.
Such to make by a human quite impossible and most unnatural.
Surely some people come across as quite peculiar.
A personality pattern quite singular!
I suggest something like heredity
and such attributes are mostly for the body.
Noting remarkable distinctions between two brothers
or between two sisters
I have heard some say and surely since times of old.
People have said, "Those two are surely not from the same mold."
One such man I heard.
The concept seemed perhaps humanly absurd.
He combed his imagination
and could come up with no explanation.
He knew only of what could come from man and the sod.
Surely he knew not Jesus, the Creator, and God.
To the natural man much shall remain obscure.

Studying the Bible, and the Trinity shall be a partial cure.
What the human begets instantly starts to waste away.
What God creates lasts like an endless day.
For many such concepts will always be an enigma.
Much for the natural man remains in the terra incognita.

Thus, to the Christian I bid.
Wonderful individualities are what Christ did.
Your life shall flourish and peak
if you let Christ be Lord and show you how you are unique.
Jesus, your Lord, can show you wonderful things not a few,
but they will remain hidden if you sinfully go askew.
Jesus can make life a fulfilling adventure.
Those obedient to Him should concur.
Unique personalities are part of every woman and man.
The Godhead designed them as part of your life's plan.

The Dr. Jekyll Factor
September 4, 1992

Surely many have heard of Dr. Jekyll and Mr. Hyde.
In utmost strangeness does much conduct abide.
In explaining much, logic does surely regress.
The brightest people also make almost no progress.
Of knowledge of angels and Satan some are void.
At the mention of them some become only annoyed.
I liken it to you explaining eternity – quite absurd
When many of you know nothing about the Word.
The many factors of the mind make the situation quite compounded.
Surely, I know why your confusion is twice confounded.
The mind is like unseen workings of wheels within wheels.
Invisible and a labyrinth the network of how one feels.
Some think the complex mind by evolution occurred.
Your nonscience religion is really absurd.
The "mere" mind alone is a high-ordered complication.
There are other factors that have an implication.
Many forces each their own exacter.
I liken some to a kind of Dr Jekyll factor.
Though the actions are quite overt,
the wherefores and wherebys are very covert.

Angels of God and angels evil always by your side.
For your entire life time they shall abide.
Angels are here and real – no doubt.
We read Jesus cast many out.

They can also read your mind and thoughts implant.
What you ordinarily think they can easily supplant.
Have you seen someone putting a temper tantrum on?
"Who pushed his hot button?"
Now you mostly know.
Hard to say exactly when and to what extent their power does go.
Evil's great influence can be obtained for a price.
To destruction like Led Zeppelin's band you also go is my advice.
Satan was their Dr. Jekyll factor which played a great role.
Were a few years of lust worth an eternity in hell for your soul?

There are also areas of the unknown that take the helm.
Mere man has little insight into this realm.
A trite level of the first is man by himself.
Angels must be at least at the level of the twelfth.
How can man explain, "Three bricks short of a load?"
We can't even see, traverse, or map the mind's road.
Many minds are also quite dysfunctional.
There is a strangeness behind behavior that is atypical.

Always unknown to man shall be some of this perplexity.
We can't see mental disease
or an influential "House of Usher" control that does not cease.
In many areas we are probing God's created infinity.
Many parts of this study are like a door that does revolve.
After going 100 times around the perplexity comes to absolutely no resolve.
All is known by God the Creator.
I must concede much to the Dr. Jekyll factor.

Instinct – A Musing
November 29, 1992

Instinct is said to be a natural aptitude.
We can find synonyms of a great plentitude.
The word did my attention demand.
There will be much to consider and the study will easily expand.
I think already that logic will be in itself an insufficient exacter.
For the natural man I suggest an additional x factor.
I have many "syns" on my list.
For a while the pondering will not desist.
Truly there are many thoughts to be diffusing.
Perhaps the circling will just all the more be confusing.

It is said to be something largely inheritable
and unalterable.

Tendency of an organism to make a complex and specific response to
environmental stimuli without involving reason too.
A behavior originating below the conscious level.
This quite well known and not unusual.
By instinct birds have the "insight"
to make their twice a year migratory flight.
The atheist would say it just somehow got there.
Their logic is just a bunch of hot air.
The atheist and agnostic have a close alliance.
Your foolish ideas are contradicted by all physics and science.
I will give you a "no never mind."
It is the innate and complex concepts I wish to expound and find.
How does one expound the exact workings of proneness?
Tell me of proclivity's inherent inclination or aptness.
Are you positive it is 100% nature
that causes tendency or is there an assistance that helps things to occur?
Consider birds returning a certain always a certain day to Capistrano.
Is it purely by natural aptitude or that they also a calendar know?
Is it solely a bird's penchant, yea, its own inclination?
Yea, atheist, guarantee me that it is entirely the bird's predisposition.
Most of the world's workings you shall never correctly diffuse
because the acceptance of God you refuse.
How can you aver that the intricate innateness
was not from the Creator and just a naturalness?
There is much to observe on propensity and behavioral bent.
For an exact atomic explanation has anyone even made a dent?

Intuition is another word that is given as a meaning.
It is the power of faculty of knowing things without conscious reasoning.
A quick and ready insight.
A second sight.
The theory the evolutionist would exert
is that all evolved upward from dirt.
Your reasoning is not just vanity,
but borders on insanity.
What evolved upward in the last 10,000 years?
Absolutely nothing it appears.
Explain exactly how the innateness came about!
It is only theories man can spout.
Who of you was there when the world was framed?
Who of you was there when the stars were hung and Orion named?
I know that God is omnipresent as a norm.
I know He is behind every gale, whirlwind, and storm.
This world is not just a nature set in motion.
God controls more than we think is my perception.
To explain how much and exactly how I cannot.
For you to deny it equally puts you on the spot.

Knowledge that God is working I have more than just received.
Those who deny God have been very deceived.
The point I make that I would have you espy
is that there is far more to everything than meets the eye.
Instinct is not a thing I was going to solve as well as ponder.
I wanted to get you to "ever the more" wonder.
Beyond man's theories and observations, you need to focus your perceptivity.
Meditation of "God in it" will be a mental walk in the high country.

An Esoteric Extrapolation
December 2, 1992

Tis sometimes amazing what is whipped up by statisticians
and what is brought out of nowhere by magicians.
Based upon what I see
I predict the economy to thus next month be.
Many examine what is only the visible temporal
and have no factor for the invisible eternal.
Merely that the world goes around and around
they can thenceforth expound.
Gathering data, the factors with their exponents
affirm the predicting theories with their proper components.
With at best a mere modification they have an answer
for a lot of things that did or will occur.
Some analysts seem to come across showing good comprehension
and thereby earn renown and recognition.
Many examiners portray the seeming fact of good perception.
The masses clamor for "the why" and the sages get a good reception.
Many imbibe to the extent of their ken.
Quite remarkable the erudition of many women and men.
Hark, hark.
Many of you are quite in the dark.
The reason for an election result seems to be thenceforth known.
You said not that elections are decided by God on the throne.
Quite incorrect you are in an esoteric extrapolation.
Evil you can see almost before you face.
Surely all can see the wicked, degenerate human race.
Upon many victims Satan has trod.
Speak of this and that there obviously must be a God.
Your theories omit too many x factors as they go.
Too surface and too temporal as to what I know.
To explain things, you sure do try.
You sure do not have a handle or theory on the why.
Your thinking needs a real reformation.
I know God because within me He has caused a transformation.

Many political analysts gave their report.
No proper "why" so I say you fall miserably short.
This life represents a short opportunity.
From there we will all be flung into eternity.
One day Satan shall undergo a great fall.
A lot of worldly theories will be totally "off the wall."
God and eternal life must be an interjection
and you will become much better with each extrapolation.

Paths and Courses Averted
February 21, 1993

Consider life's many goings
and meanderings.
Often life for some is opting many options.
Selections are made by chance, facts, desires, and predilections.
Consider where you are today.
What major choices made things come this way?
Certainly for a job that was given
did many things thusly and thereby "shapen."
Suppose you had gone to a different city.
There is a supposition beyond human predictability.

Suppose a spouse was selected one courtship sooner
or had it tarried to one courtship later.
In this you surely know
that things would really differently go.
Genetics and offspring.
Now for that is an unimaginable thing.
So bewildering that to a certain one I could not pledge.
My mouth was stopped by God is my present knowledge.
My mind often refocused to keep us at a standstill.
God accomplished his will.

Thus, to predict every non-opted path
is far more than high level math.
Oh, but God looked ahead.
By His choice we were led.
His children are coursed by a careful determination.
Lady Luck has nothing to do with our destination.
There are many things in life to make us really ponder.
Over a few things you must surely wonder.
Know that when you get to glory
God can unfold all in a visual story.
He can show you what life would have been on each road not taken.

In many cases by His choice we were disappointed, but not forsaken.
Only for God is this something He can easily show.
He would be deciding things here too as things would go.

If you are a child of the King,
you were opted for a better thing.
Over not getting things many have surely cried.
In an attempt of attainment much effort was tried.
For all things you need to wonder about God's power.
He will show you everything at the appointed hour.

(This poem in intended to get you to think about God's infinite
knowledge. Spouse, city you live in, church, and place you work are
only illustrations of what could have changed in your life. God
can one day show you how life "would have been." He is able)

The Web
July 19 & 20, 1996

Look to nature to make you additionally wise.
The scripture and Proverbs exhort, so this is no surprise.
Consider the spider's web in spiritual levels of two.
As an enhancement of wisdom this will surely do.
No, wait, there will be three.
A tad more of contemplation yielded this you will shortly agree.
You will truly enter insight's door
if you can refract this into levels of four.
That can't come in a flash, you need hesitate.
Pray, think, ponder, and really contemplate.
As the poet you may need to put the pen to flight
and only see upon reflection the truth and insight.

Our Christian relationships is the topic sure.
This is what the web is to picture.
I meditated and saw four!
Now insight and wisdom can grow a bit more.
Arrive in paths of two.
Your self-meditation or a further reading will do.
Before you really read on,
your own thinking hat is what you should don.

Follow on ye who for wisdom and knowledge thirst.
Consider now level of the first.
Christians moving to and fro.
A few we meet and thereby know.

Some we see in a certain here
will also show up in some other there.
Thus, we go traversing the web and the world
until off into eternity we are hurled.
For relationships or else some do no further search.
They will not get beyond a greeting in a church.
Some money in a plate is also nice.
Now just to end here for many will not suffice.

Level two is where most do go.
Much could be written I surely know.
But you know that in poetic verse
we shall be terse.
The gifted saints are put together for edification.
Are you involved? Give it some meditation.
Are you sensitive to others' needs?
We are exhorted to do good deeds.
It can be a ministry to use your pen.
For needs the Lord reveals the what and the when.
To hear of a missionary or m.k. getting something "just in time"
is quite rewarding and goes way beyond the mere attendee's mime.
For some the credit card is loose and the budget is really tight.
By having no extra you will lose many a delight.
Another may have a woe and you they need to hear.
Words from God can "into your mouth" appear.
It should by practice and knowledge be a rule.
If you are available, you can be the Master's tool.
By now it should be plain
that we are working on a web of a higher plane.
This is level number two.
You who stay on level one shall someday rue.
I wrote previously of trekking in the high country.
Here one does behold more magnificence and beauty.

Now first I saw one, two, and three.
This is the physical and spiritual working generally.
Level three became four
as I saw one more.
More important is the role
of the Most High who is in total control.
Much of our workings and direction
occur by His help and purposeful intervention.
Now if it were six levels at which we did stop
God will always be "level of the top."
We sometimes can't tell what was our choice
or whether God did nudge or directly inspire our voice.
So, picture now a two-tiered web and nigh

it and in control, of course, is the Most High. (level four)

So thus we saw what was more visibly
easy to picture, imagine, and see.
Now run this through insight's prism
to refract the last to add to your wisdom.
Some may not have a clue or trace.
The fact of the fourth is dangling in front of your face.
The simple end or our search
is that we are one in Christ, the church. (level three)
This is like an invisible web, a oneness.
Visibly the least, but spiritually, a sureness.
Thus, another example of how by insight
the invisible solidifies into a picture to our delight.
There are the four.
For now, we will say no more.

"The Web" Revisited
April 14, 1999

"The Web" is a good instruction to review.
Many carnal Christians that do nothing are gone askew.
So easy to see is level of the first.
Many just eat, meet, greet, and only notably then the Hearst.

For some needy people there are things we can do.
Add this and you progress to level two.
Good to show we care
by some things we share.
This giving can remain simple and plain.
Ah, Christian, you should progress to the next plane.

Than to anonymously give you can do better.
Share, care, talk, pray, and perhaps send a letter.
Consider that you pen is relatively light.
It will put you on a more fulfilled spiritual flight.
Similarly, for other things of the Lord you should ask.
Many things can be done that make not at all a difficult task.
Consider that many will be robbed by the devil
if he can prevent them from coming to this level.
Let us call this level three.
The better spiritual walk you should agree.

"The Web" described connections and relationships.
Meeting others by communications and trips.

The physical things have themselves a simple role.
Level of the highest is God in control.
He is the web's master spinner.
Get on Christian and you become a winner.
Give your spiritual life great consideration with due circumspect.
Far better off you will be if you intently walk.

Circumspect: adj. Careful to consider all circumstances and
    consequences, prudent.

Life
August 15, 2016

To write about life,
the narrowing down alone could cause much strife.
For many learning is a delight.
I go beyond knowledge and facts with "insight."
Two poems to your reading you should add.
Academicians could be quite glad.
(Poems are: "Oh, For Wisdom and Discernment" and "Gaining Insight")

Much of our life was striving for balance.
That was mostly pain and practice - little came by chance.
Charity, tithe yourself (retirement), homes, cars, and vacation make a
    Important list.
Give attention to all five – do not resist.
Putting way too much into three and four
will cause one, two, and five to be a situation to deplore.
Where did you travel to and what did you see?
Payments too high – we could only go to McDee.
Most have quite limited resources.
They cannot do well in all five courses.
Perhaps we should have all learned to walk a tightrope.
Then maybe "balance" would always be in mind I would hope.
The soon you learn this in life
will proportionately reduce a lot of strife.
While in Dallas I was a Financial Director.
On interest, compounding, and the above five to some I was an instructor.
Hope you were like me – passed on what I knew.
Help others avoid disasters or going unnecessarily askew.

Desideratum
March 10, 1991

Oh world, you have a need.
It is not more instruction to fulfill your greed.
Though you do well at getting to the financial top,
it will all one day stop.
Consider your course in this world.
To where then shall you be hurled?
The soul and the resurrected body shall live forever.
Your final state shall change "never."
Today you set your course.
Be sure it is not one to cause remorse.
Oh world, you have a need.
The Word of God is the required seed.
Jesus Christ is the savior you need.
For your sins and mine He did bleed.
As your savior you must accept Him and salvation embrace
or else you will run the wrong course and race!

Oh saint, you have a need.
You must learn, grow, and the Word evermore read.
We need to get to the spiritual top
before our life does stop.
Consider your course in the world.
Are your desires upon the proper things furled?
We know we shall live forever.
Heaven's final state must be today's endeavor.
Today we shall set our eternal course.
Some things shall surely cause remorse.
We indeed have a need.
Obedience to the word of God is the seed.
Jesus Christ for daily living is what we need.
For all to accept Him He did die and bleed.
As our Lord and daily provider, He is the one to embrace.
Report for duty or else you will run the wrong course!

(Desideratum: [Latin] something desired as essential or needed.)

Fronti Nulla Fides
March 10, 1991

There is a way that seems right,
but the end shall lead to a terrible plight.
"Believe nothing you hear and only half of what you see."
I heard this way back in years that never again shall be.
You had better agree
that there is much more than what we see.
Death has for all a role,
but man can't see the spirit or soul.
One third of heaven was cast down.
You see not a form, smile, or frown.
Angels to all people have their assignment.
So partly rejoice and partly lament.
For alcohol or drugs do you have a passion?
The lust and desire are all of evil fashion.
The body stupid has no preference for drink.
It is only mental that people imbibe beyond their brink.
How about gluttonous, ravenous for sweets?
The body stupid wants only nutrition (not stupid) - not sugar or meats.
So, before you is just empty space?
God stands with the angels right in front of your face!
For all He has many commands.
The situation surely demands.
Almost nothing is just simply "as it seems."
But so, the fool dreams.
One saw just a man to look upon King Midas.
So surely "fronti nulla fides."
(The body may have some desires or addictions, but that is
small compared to fired up desires and lusts.)
(Fronti nulla fides. [Latin] no reliance can be placed upon appearance.)

Non Sum Qualis Eram
March 12, 1991

Since twenty years ago I have changed.
Many things have been rearranged.
A new life since seventy two.
The changes are not yet through.
This new life yet less than one score.
New learning to replace old lore.
A savior taken to heart.
New things the Lord does impart.

Saith scripture we are to grow.
More of Jesus we are to know.
It is the power of the divine source
that has me traverse a different course.

A new birth should show.
Some or many habits need to oft go.
A Christian life has a special design.
The world should see an evidential sign.
A changed life all should see!
That evidences sanctification you should agree.
Are you a Christian by name?
Your life had better not be the same.
There would be reason to shed some tears
if it changed not over the years.
As one to the Lord draws nearer,
the Lord Jesus and His work should be dearer.
Upon your change and progress, you should reflect.
A charge of "still the same" better not be correct.
Indeed, a new creature I am.
Non sum quails eram!

(Non sum quails eram: [Latin]: I am not what I used to be.)

Abeunt Studia in Morés
March 15, 1991

Consider the many things you should do.
List also some avoidances and some things to rue.
What you hate, evil would have you do.
They resist you on virtuous things too.
Consider a few things – "these I must."
Let me flee temptation and things of lust.

Slow starters there are aplenty.
The do-littles are in great quantity.
Read again and again that which is good.
"I shall do the things I should."
"As a man thinketh, so he is."
Studying values and morés is a super biz.

Read and grasp the holy light.
Such study is the Lord's delight.
Light sought turns into light found.
Consider a course to which you should be bound.

Failure shall mount from habits of flagrancy.
The secret of success is consistency.

Write a list and work the list.
Note the things later you missed.
Teach children to do good little deeds.
Teach them to help with people's needs.
"Did you do a good deed today?"
"Do you read the Word every day and pray?"
Striving to do a good or right thing pays.
Practicing good habits form good morés.
(Abeunt studia in morés: [Latin] Practices zealously pursued
pass into habits.)

Aequam Servare Mentem
March 16, 1991

Oh, what trouble in the world and all around.
What worldly things are reliable or sound?
War is always at hand.
Selfish people always trying to fulfill every demand.
If it would only be mere strife
to course the ways of life!
The country has more debt than it should bear.
To pile on more is all the mad politicians care.
We are reaping the reward for wickedness and sin.
Only for a multitude on their knees will elsewhere begin.
Slay the unborn and let the mad killer dictator go free.
Justice is gone awry and perverse you should agree.
All consequences have their reason.
See now the result of "sin for a season."
Sin shall accomplish much in its quest.
We can never see again great rest.
The wicked shall never repent.
Evil rejoices more as the saints ever the more lament.
Oh, wicked suffering humanity.
You give nothing to preserve one's sanity.

Wickedness does God allow.
He preserves the praying saints even now.
God is my rest.
Oh, world events, you give me nothing but misery and unrest.
Evil emanates their fruit in an appalling flood.
Praise the Lord, my sins are covered by the blood.
Part of me has peace amid the storm.

This shall continue to be my norm.
I am a sojourner on the way to a better place.
I know the resultant of the world's wicked pace.
Into Sheol you shall go down.
You will rue with far more than a sad frown.
The world gives me no peace of mind.
Only God is able "to preserve a calm mind."
(Aequam servare mentem [Latin]: To preserve a calm mind.)

Ehu Fugaces Labuntur Anni

March 16, 1991

The more I reflect the more time has fled.
The grass does quickly wither it was said.
For what shall all my labor count?
For whom after shall all my goods mount?
What is done for Christ it has also been said
shall count for a reward that goes on ahead.
Small deeds here is the leaven
that builds up treasures in heaven.
Life does so quickly while away.
For a special reason I was meant a time to stay.
The day (life) is now past noon.
The end of life may come very soon.
Lord, let my service quickly abound.
With just a few rewards I wish not to be found.
Acquiring goods can be a consuming pace.
Nay, this was not the intent of my race.
Too many shall have many tears
realizing they whiled away the years.
Not by just those saved at the eleventh hour.
For a few the course of Christian service went sour.
Many shall realize the unpleasant fate
that will befall because they remained in a carnal state.
The best and only true reward
comes from living life in tune with the Lord.
For life I could never realize richness and deepness.
Only God gives eternal perspective and meaningfulness.
With the title you should agree.
Ehu fugaces labunter anni.
(Ehue fagaces labunter anni [Latin]: Alas, the fleeting years glide on.)

De Minimis Non Curat Lex
March 27, 1991

Do you think you should
get to heaven because you are good?
There are two ways I suggest.
One should be the best.
To the law we are all subject.
We get to heaven by being perfect!

So many think they will get to heaven by living the law.
Did you know you had to fulfill it without a flaw?
Your demerit sheet must be without any specks.
De minimis non curat lex.
To earn your way on things can sure appall.
If you are guilty of one point, you are guilty of all.
To subject yourself to the law has a cost.
By it all would elsewise be lost.

From the power that sent the flood
can also provide plenty of Christ's "sin's covering blood."
This easy way to salvation you can easily partake.
No better way can you ever make.
Death and the afterlife are out of your hands.
All human hopes are but dunes of sinking sands.
For death man has no cure.
Be covered by the blood and be absolutely sure.

(De minimis non curat lex [Latin]: The law takes no account of trifles.)

Vae Victis
April 27, 1991

For most across the land
they are victims of the battle at hand.
You are become vanquished by your ignorance.
"You don't know the half of it," is your state of cognizance.
The New Age and evil to some are an interesting dabble.
Many will be reduced to rubble.
You who toy with such, play, and dally
shall become victims of your own folly.
Can you trifle with something a thousand times your might?
Assuredly the learned can predict your plight.
Satan and his force

will deliver you only a ruinous course.
Is the board or a seer a thing you admire?
Their power wishes you to accompany them in the eternal fire.
Two powers are opting you to their kingdom.
Fear of the eternal marks the beginning of wisdom.
You who normally try to reduce strife and sorrow,
think twice of what could occur on the morrow.
This earth has much evil ground to easily hoe.
To you who are overcome, woe, woe, woe!

Though Christ is your master,
you can also err and bring mental and physical disaster.
You are not in an invulnerable state.
Your smugness will deliver you a partial fate.
Christ and the Word need be your armor and shield.
You'll never do well alone on Satan's field.
Christ and God are the infinite power.
Satan is the deceiver who is at hand to devour.
Perhaps some (or much) ground you did cede.
To Christ, His Word, and victory you must proceed.
Learn of Christ, His Word, and its power you will see and feel.
Satan wants you to think it nonsense that he wishes to conceal.
Armstrong's "The Bondage Breaker" has much to proclaim.
It shows the power of Christ as something we can claim.
Woe to you if by Satan you are vanquished,
but by the power of Christ it will be relinquished.
Satan will not easily go and you will feel the pains of withdrawal.
Victory will occur if Christ is your Master and wherewithal.

(Vae Victus / wi wik tes/ [Latin]: Woe to the vanquished.)

Ultima Ratio Regum
June 21, 1991

We know of the powers on high.
Neither side man can defy.
Evil seems to come ever more to full bloom.
Surely more and more are coming to ruin and doom.
Certain of us the gospel does defend.
The enemy wishes to bring it to an end.
The conflict seems to increase.
There shall be no lasting worldly peace.
No utopia shall evolve from our present state.
Many shall encounter their fate.

Some doves think they will succeed in their task.
"What shall be the end of it," others do ask.
God and His angels work amid triumph and doom.
Nefarious specters loom.
All spirits must to God and Jesus obey.
All take instructions every day.
Satan can only thrive
because fools submit to his jive.
Many actually worship him as someone so great.
He is dragging them along to his terrible fate.
One day this present battle to an end shall come.
Armageddon – ultima ratio regum!

(Ultima ratio regum [Latin]: The final argument of kings, i.e. war)

In Hoc Signo Vinces
June 23, 1991

Contemplate the much to be done
and the souls to be won.
Go not on just wit and wisdom.
Will many be added to the Lord's kingdom?
A foolish general will quickly charge
and see he is no match for the powers at large.
Know you of whose armor you should be clad?
Oh soldier, you will be defeated or glad.

Some will be quite pugnacious or bold
to conquer for more gold.
Though rich there will be a great cost
when they discover they were all the while lost.
From the physical and worldly you need to turn.
There are better things to yearn.
To make evil retreat and wince shall produce glorious battle days.
We need the power of God us to amaze.
In hoc signo vinces.

(In hoc signo Vinces [Latin]: By this sign (the cross) you will conquer.)

O Tempora! O Mores!
October 3, 1991

Alas, the times!
The righteous go through almost helpless mimes.
The wicked do greatly flourish.
Insatiable desires do so many feed and nourish.
Lo and behold, what is the world's course?
The empowering dragon is indeed its source.
The economy and morality are in a dive.
Lest you turn about world, you will not revive
to a state of health
or enjoy an otherwise earned wealth.

O gambler, do not even think to bet
whether God's wrath is showing up in national debt.
This country is trying to spend its way to prosperity,
but I see only mounds of debt and near total bankruptcy.
The perverted are being upheld by man's law.
It is no small evil or flaw.
Most are doing what feels right
and going after it with all of their might.
So, in merriment and in revelry you sing.
The foolish do forget death shall impose its sting.

Think upon what is right, wrong, or absurd.
God surely "has the last word."
All will be measured against God's righteousness too.
Is this what Jesus would do?
That question must always be in the forefront.
The crowd opposingly shall inflict consequential brunt.
Ten spies to the promised land caused Israel's plight.
It proves the majority is not always right.
These present deeds shall bring upon us more evil days.
O tempora! O mores!

(O tempora! O mores! [Latin]: Oh, the times! Oh, the manners!)

Uno Amino
October 5, 1991

Oh, perilous and strife filled days.
A product of sin bound and selfish bent ways.
Consider the aspect of the mental state.

That is, the goals we are seeking is the point to deliberate.
For truth and justice each has a different mind.
No consensus or reconciliation can anyone find.
So, who is to blame
that most are not of the same mental frame?
A model all were given to meditate upon,
but Christ for most is nothing to think on.

The cure of sin's consequences you have despised.
The coming downfall shall be worse than could be surmised.
Man's state and welfare are things of evermore deterioration.
Both economics and virtue are headed to extermination.
Turn to Christ before you become totally destitute.
In full surrender to Him you must be resolute.
To know and serve Christ must be our only goal.
God could then heal this land and make it whole.
A solution to the world's woes you can find
if you look totally to Jesus with one mind.

[Latin: uno amino – with one mind]
Tempora Mutantur, Nos et Mutamur in Illis
October 6, 1991

I oft looked at sin and degradation.
World, you are thrusting yourself into destruction.
Science and knowledge are evermore.
The state of man is one to deplore.
A sad picture the mirror of reality paints.
Then I ponder the state of the saints.
Oh church, you are not remaining in purity and separation.
Being in the world and not of it was not to be an option.
Lusts, worldly music, and selfishness have invaded Christendom.
Shall Christ be ever proud of such a kingdom?
Must Christ's return be one God needs to hasten
because the church can no one properly chasten?
Of Christ's loyal, holy order are you yet fit?
Worldly goals will cause you to make an unwise gambit.
Some codes of holiness will be near impossible to instill
if your morals are like the world's rolling down the hill.
Be not like salt that has lost its savor.
The church can't risk losing favor.
Swaying to a wicked world is departing from our first love.
A compromising church can't be tolerated by Christ above.
Beware church lest Christ reacts because He is jealous.

Tempora mutantur, nos et mutamur in illis.

(tempora mutantur, nos et mutamur in illis [Latin]: the times are changing, and we are changing with them.)

Suaviter in Modo, Fortiter in re
October 9, 1991

How quickly people do war or clash
or reach out in a swiping lash.
Some virtues were handed down from above.
You warring, man was taught to love.
Too many do demand
that they rule with an iron hand.
Peacemakers are sought for their utility.
Their efforts often end in futility.
From God's way and teaching you did depart.
Therefore, no peace will He impart.
You have gone down your own path.
Your sinful ways shall reap much wrath.
On your humanistic endeavors you are bent.
Oh, what a difference if you would repent.

God makes the lion lie down with the lamb we read.
He performs a miracle where man can only do a deficient deed.
It is God who alters even one's character.
Man does little better than draw a caricature.
By man much wasted effort is wrought.
To accomplish little, you are rightly thereby distraught.
Debt and spending will remain out of control
because your destiny has a Godless role.
He is the one causing all of your ills.
He unleashes the evil force churning their destruction mills.
If it were in Jesus you did abide,
It would be totally different with Him on your side.
Without a doubt
there is much you would carry out.
Jesus changes the hearts of men.
The child could play by the adder's den.
Good things from His bounty He would give
and show all how they could peacefully live.
With Jesus peace and prosperity would succeed.
We would just walk gently in manner, strongly in deed.

[Latin: suaviter in modo, fortiter in re – gently in manner, strongly in deed]

Se Non E Vero, E. Ben Trovato

October 9, 1991

Know thine adversary you have been told.
On this you need well lay hold.
The lie by cunning and guile he did conceive.
His will is to destroy or deceive.
He purports that the best of life is lust or some virtuous similitude.
He exerts by the utmost allowed magnitude.
He does not wander around flittering in a mime.
The evil force is at work full-time.
My quill can't pen
how much he knows about all women and men.
He will not just fool you once.
Satan is no dunce.
Plotting, not in madness, just in evil sanity
the destruction of humanity.
Do you wish sensation and lust?
He will cause your morals to go totally bust.
Else you be a high-minded philosopher,
he is ever much more.
His force can best you in logic, cruel humanity,
mind games, wisdom, deception, or any improbity.

Behind every sin there is a lie.
"You may eat of the tree of life and not die."
Some type of trap evil will set
or of God's law they will cause you to forget.
They will blind you to the fact of the morrow
after a sinful deed or life will cause only sorrow.
Evil can sully the highest knowledge of men – their's being superficial.
This is a fact – a statement not at all prejudicial.
Of eternity and consequences, you need to be aware.
Alone without Christ against Satan you will always woefully fare.
Sooner or later you will feel the brunt.
Every sinful appeal is a false front.
Se non e vero,
E. ben trovato.

[Italian: even if it is not true, it is well conceived.]

Sic Iter ad Astra
October 10, 1991

Orbiting astronauts were really only a few.
Around the earth not many flew.
But, wow, what a view!
Only Apollo 13 went askew.
(You are not superstitious, are you?)
For excellence a moon landing will do.
To other planets camera only rockets went in lieu
of mankind you also knew.

To other planets they went.
On a short trek on the way to the stars they were sent.
On space exploration man is desirously bent.
In accruing knowledge of them he has not even made a dent.
A fact a knowledge seeker does resent
is that a lifetime to many in travel would be spent.
Most can only pitch a tent
and dream when they look at the night stars that it is there they went.

Thus, the foe of star travel would be mortality.
Self-imposed immortality
is met with futility.
Never successful even though approached with all fidelity!
A trip through the black hole in the stars can be a surety
only if it is Christ taking you to heaven's eternity.
Belief and trust in Christ can put you in His eternal loving custody.
Thus, one goes to the stars; such is the way to immortality.

[Latin: sic iter ad astra – thus one goes to the stars, such is the way to immortality.]

Sic Semper Tyrannis
October 12, 1991

A phrase came up in a debate.
It became a motto of a state.
Tyrants were deplored.
Where such, freedom and righteousness need to be restored.
Good and evil today are rising in hot debate.
Evil loved by some, by others a thing they do viciously hate.

Choose whom you will serve.
In the end you will get what you deserve.

Above all it is God whom you should fear.
The destiny of your soul ought to be very dear.
The things of God do the majority spite.
Consider what could be in sight.

Oh, today a terrible battle does rage.
It seems to be setting a stage.
Mankind is running down a destructive path.
Great sin invariably brings about God's judgmental wrath.
Oh, how we need a spiritual revival.
It is almost now necessary for survival.

Oh, how people need to pray.
Only God can turn hearts this or any day.
By the Holy Spirit people need to be (yielded) filled.
The power of sin needs to be stilled.
On great wickedness people seem by and large bent.
Think what could happen if people would greatly repent.

Judgment or revival the situation does shortly demand.
Only God knows what could happen across our land.
Satan, tyrants, tyranny, and evil need to be rejected.
Praying saints, we have reason to be "abjected."
To see evil suppressed and righteousness raised will cause much bliss.
Sic semper tyrannis.

[Latin: sic semper tyrannis – thus ever to tyrants – motto of Virginia]

Sic Transit Gloria Mundi
October 12, 1991

Most work or trade to earn.
We know of the innate desire to yearn.
Work and time gain more and more.
Some gain little but toil until they are sore.
Others with talents "much"
procure accordingly such.
The elders are to lay in store I read.
For some it seems like it "has gone to their head."
Indeed, they have much wealth in store.
Their moral state is often one to deplore.
Consider each trying to pile up more than his brother.
Alas, you will die and leave it to another.
Time will eventually sap your health
and then what good will be your wealth?

For many wealth has its pull and gravity.
Are you not in abject depravity?
Those who use it to glorify the Lord
shall gain an eternal reward.
What is a petty life out of one billion years?
The evil destined will have eons to shed some tears
and to no avail.
Set your course now while the breath of life can alter your sail.
Pity some can't amass enough to make their kingdom whole.
What does it profit to gain the whole world and lose your soul?

[Latin: sic transit gloria mundi – so passes away the glory of the world]

Age Quod Agis
October 31, 1991

Upon the Lord we surely wait.
We reflect upon many years of our state.
We tried hard and oft to venture out.
A lot of frustration too, no doubt.
Part of life was a purposeful mime,
but amid thus were lessons learned over time.
To leave was a must.
Determined as the wagoners, "California or bust."
A waiting ordained by God one can't avoid.
We had many tears of dryness and a certain void.
It never really became better we did time after time learn.
It would one day change we did also discern.
Certainly, a path never totally barren.
We learned many things whereby and wherein.
So hard to believe this long purposeful wait.
We found ever more hope in spite of the state.
To believe we would leave we continued to dare.
We knew that the Lord did greatly care.
To go we could only pray and not demand.
Where would be this future perhaps nether land?
Surely would come the day
that revealed it would be far away.
Pondering the mystery was an almost deliriousness.
Always at the forefront was a confirmatory sureness.
Verses of promise came to assure and attest.
The long wait was the difficult bear against whom we had to wrest.
Times of convincing sureness were at lack,
but we were directed down this track.
What else, but go on as is.

The Lord answered, "Age quod agis."

[Latin: age quod agis – do what you are doing, to the business at hand.]

Salus Populi Suprema Lex Esto
December 20, 1991

That the greatest command is obeyed is hereby an assumption.
Then on the second goes our continuation.
It would be to all well,
if they would meditate upon this a spell.
The phrase stresses others.
One is not to seek lordship of self above his brothers.
We know many are evil and will inflict any pain
needful of arriving at their gain.
It is love to seek the general welfare
of others and to show we care.
A worldly kingdom of Christ we do not observe.
He came as the humble one and thereby to serve.
It was sacrificial of self and humanly a positional loss
for Christ to die and suffer on the cross.
He taught his disciples to care.
Their possessions with others they did share.
The concept of love
unto others came down from above.
He is no fool
who wishes to obey the golden rule.
One should not need a reminder or prod
that all things are considered by God.
There was a principle Jesus did decree.
"He who does things unto the least does them unto me."
Seeking the welfare of others shall earn its reward.
For such is "of the Lord."

[Salus populi suprema lex esto (Latin): Let the welfare of the people be
the supreme law – motto of Missouri]

Respice finem
December 22, 1991

What a poor woman or man
who does not at all plan.

You have absolutely no wisdom
if you consider not your subsequent eternal kingdom.
For some their ignorance is erroneously arrogant
in that they think not that something will be resultant.
The temptation of sin is a lie.
"Eat of the fruit, you will surely not die."
Many sins the evil host can successfully beget
in that the fact of the consequences they make you forget.

Consider he who has built for 25 years and many a day.
If your heart becomes prideful, the Lord may take it all away.
Though you then repent and get "on track,"
you can never get the loss back.
Solomon's temple was magnificent and grand.
The praise of excellence it did surely demand.
With sin and wickedness, the people more than toyed.
The people were carried away and the temple was destroyed.
The fear of God, Cyrus, king of Persia, did espouse.
The Lord charged him to send a remnant back to build a house.
A few aged remembered Solomon's temple and Jerusalem's wall.
The new temple was going to be comparatively inferior, trite, and small.
The foolish people considered not the fruit of "sin for a season."
Blinded sinners seem void of any logic or ability to reason.
If the Lord takes away 25 years of toil and labor,
your repentance may never cause your wealth to reoccur.

Know you not that our work has eternal consequence?
For all deeds or good works shall have due recompense.
Why would one needlessly sorrow
because he considered not the reward coming tomorrow?
Pondering the consequences of tomorrow your planning should stem.
Respice finem.

[respice finem (Latin): look to the end, consider the outcome.)

Re Infecta

December 22, 1991

Perhaps many can mull, "Consider what I am
I am far from perfection and closer to a sham."
Growing in the Lord is a long, tedious strife.
The Lord intends to use our entire life.
To all other saints we need to carefully look.
As they yet live, none are a "finished book."
Many in their current state

are suspect and can stir up much debate.
After years some seem still so close to their previous unruly hour.
Know that they can only change by the Lord's power.
For rewards many shall not progress to a desirable fate.
Nay, all too many shall remain in a carnal state.
We can only speak, exhort, teach, and pray.
Results are the Lord's doing and on His appointed day.
One can only exert an imaginative vista.
Nearly always – re infecta.

Consider also our business at hand.
Are some needful finishes in demand?
Do you know some people who have a lot of loose ends hanging?
Are too many things going and completion coming to nothing?
Reflect upon your spiritual, business, and daily state.
Perhaps you need prioritize things on a slate.
There are numerous activities galore to desire.
Before you know it, you can have too many irons in the fire.
Every sailing ship must have its proper manning.
There must be some beforehand planning and present examining.
"Keep short accounts." I heard one pastor say.
That was a gem of a thought for the day.
So, through life we need to progress
or upon death your spouse and kin will have a mess.
Give the present state of your affairs a proper review
lest in neglect you and they both go askew.
Take stock or your life will be simultaneously running circus arena.
Too much could come to re infecta.

(re infecta [Latin]: the business being unfinished.)

Absit Invidia
December 25, 1991

Talents and possessions of others you see many.
One can't help but almost surely "take inventory."
Then naturally comes the report
of whether you are way ahead or quite short.
Tis natural the accumulations of possessions.
Pity for some that attainment translates into obsessions.
Then must one to another tell
of the Christian neighbor's abode how so-so or how swell?
God has Christians in huts that are thatched.
as well as colonial manors with furniture and drapes well-matched.
Some who endure great adversity and lose it all

will have for eternity blessings and rewards quite tall.
Stop letting earthly things from being any type of measure.
Invisible are daily inner joy and labor for eternal treasure.
If you go to a distant town for a meeting to be spiritually ahead,
just be thankful for anyone lending a bed.
Though one have a manor for a house,
as a Christian testimony they may be a louse.
Invisible will be the reward of obedience to God,
but it should be manifested by the public and political ground one does trod.
Abilities and talents come from the Creator.
Of the affluent gain of others, we are not to be an envier.
Working for gain will be a normal topic of debate.
"Lord, make me content in my present state."
Evil via an "envy trip" can really take you for a ride.
One's focus must be stayed upon Jehovah you must decide.
To insert your mind with lust, pride, or envy evil will plot.
Then one does evaluate his lot.
"Divide and conquer" is Satan's goal.
They attempt to fracture the church to be not whole.
A mind stayed upon the Lord's desirous path
will take the steam out of the results of Satan's wrath.
Looking too critically upon another's error or goods can lead to a dilemma.
So, I exhort, "Absit Invidia."

(Absit Invidia [Latin]: Let there be no envy or ill will)

Nil Desperandum
December 25, 1991

Some seemed doomed to a terrible fate.
Yea, very lamentable is their state.
Our woes never seem to dissolve.
No solution comes either by utmost resolve.
So, if no turning no matter how hard you try,
consider the situation intact by the power on high.
All of the universe must obey the triune God's command.
All is in control that occurs "at hand."
Though we sadly cry a lot of tears,
we must continue in prayer for all of our years.
A focus on God is a must.
He alone is the confidence of our trust.
There will be times when much is overpowering and wrong.
Singing the moody blues will seem the only appropriate song.
For both sin and the virtues of Job can one have great pain.
We know not what is God's intended gain.

Many things of God's plan for us are made known.
There are also many things of Him that shall remain unknown.
For the situations we can't repair
are the ones that will surely cause despair.
It seems there are some hurting already many seasons
and have no revealed reasons.
In misery only shall not all of one's life be spent.
"God wishes all to have an expected end," is well meant.
Though you seem at the end of your rope,
in God yet must you hope.
Trusting the God of all power
shall give unto you a redeeming hour.
Only because He is all powerful can our faith have no maximum.
Nil desperandum

(nil desperandum [Latin}: never despair)

Non Omnia Possumus Omnes
December 30, 1991

Some things of the flesh and mind are variable
and others are more fixed and unmodifiable.
So, consider that which is hard to change
or what seems you can't rearrange.
Though the mind and body each seem to have some stretch,
a few who can't outstretch the most seem a mental wretch.
Everyone can't be the best
and always above the rest.
A few want to be better than everyone
and are distraught when not every event is won.
You should conclusively find
that such a person is in a rather unhealthy state of mind.
Some will "by all means"
be the one going to the extremes.

It is fun and excellent to compete,
but you graciously need to know how to accept defeat.
One parent told her daughter it was all college A's she should have.
Anything less would come across as a lazy knave.
Not being perfect caused more than strife.
The gal tried to take her own life!
There needs to be some time for leisurely zest.
One can't be burned up becoming the best.
Everything must be done in reasonable moderation,
though a few times and events could require much practice before competition.

But consider all of your duties and each role
before you go all-out to obtain a goal.
You have gone too far to sacrifice a daily devotion
because it was necessary in the quest of your ambition.
Though a certain thing you would admire,
let it not become a consuming fire.
(It would be another thing to discuss what could be done for the Lord
and how He would enable you to earn a mighty reward.)
Let nothing go beyond a reasonable role
or it shall take an undesirable toll.
It is difficult to go beyond the ostensible joy success brings.
We need remember, "We can't all do all things."

(non omnia possumus omnes [Latin]: We can't all do all things.)

Natura Non Facit Saltum
February 2, 1992

Oh, how oft do things creep
instead of making our desired quantum leap.
Perhaps a new soul into the fold,
but not too soon sanctified and bold.
Some bad habits seem to never die.
Some deeds that a testimony belie.
Why must growth sometimes move like a snail?
It seems a few will die before they get to the end of the trail.
(Sadly, we know some will counter inspire
in that they shall only be saved from the fire.
Their growth immediately goes on pause
and they shall never enhance the Christian cause.
Thus, on some we must sadly conclude.
This topic I now shall exclude.)

As a child does very slowly grow,
so the spiritual ascension also seems to be slow.
The pace is not by human design.
The spiritual gait does the Father allot and assign.
The bumps along the ride
were not for evil to plan and decide.
Thus, because we love peace and hate misery,
we do not plan too well for eternity.
Thus, in God we can take hope.
The spiritual oscillates on a higher, more invisible scope.
Know that in spiritual matters your mind can ascend.
The natural mind and the spiritual have a different trajectory.

Oh, how rewarding it will be to walk in the "high country."
Did not Half Dome take much time to gain
and cause one to experience and endure some pain?
Since we can't see the beauty of where we are going,
most do not opt a hasty coursing.
Only from the mountain can one get the full view.
Evil purpose is to keep you down and make you go askew.
You have heard, "Desire determines destination."
Know that God is doing the spiritual conveyance and transition.
One can do no better than will.
The prescription is one only God can fill.
We may only see our pace going like a rill.
Unless one is preoccupied by sin, he is not standing still.
It is not God's way to have you do 10 g's in a power climb
and immediately be spiritually sublime.
Thus, we need to learn more patience along the way.
The earth was not built either in one day.

(natura non facit saltum [Latin]: nature makes no leaps.)

Quorum Pars Magna Fui
February 2, 1992

Contemplate your each and every role.
Perhaps some turn out well and others take a toll.
For some as the prerequisite is increasing smarts,
accomplishment quickly departs.
Some can influence others by great charisma
and they can easily persuade in their forth put dogma.
What power do we have to advance morality
or outrightly benefit humanity?
Reflect the degree you exact spiritual progress.
Of such I can only think, "I, the Less."

Now most Christians do find
that God has for them a purpose in mind.
Yea, surely there can be many tears
as the unknown purpose will come only after many years.
Dissatisfaction can be gripping at the heart
before God reveals that some shall depart.
Every time you reflect and pause
everything seems to come up a lost cause.
Thus, it is God who controls stagnation
or who quickly courses one to completion.
One can surely get a fulfilling thrill

to see everything going as easily as "rolling down the hill.
The God who causes frustration or hope
is also the one who changes the slope.
Who created the molehill and well as the mountain?
Only from an infinite, energetic fountain!

In much I realize I only do through a mime
as it is of God's doing all of the time.
So not so much as what I touch
as God causes accomplishment little or much.
A realization we all need
is that we can only alter our "to and fro" walking speed.
In that I merely am a being to which God can impart,
it is only that in which I played a great part.

(quorum pars magna fui [Latin]: in which I played a great part.)

Paucis Verbis
February 2, 1992

Be it something I once heard of or read
or something that just came into my head,
I expound
until time's end or no more ideas are found.
To my state of knowledge by time I have been led.
I am often reflecting upon or digesting what I have been fed.
I need to have enough lead I know
and I just pen my mind's flow.
It shall never be exclusively just my soul.
The triune God and angels each play a role.
I hear three words and from here I am coming,
but oft I know not where it is going.
Then finally before my eyes
turns out a pleasant surprise.

What a strange new parallelism!
A new form penned for an old ism.
Reflection is an enjoyable time.
Three paragraphs of eight with each keeping the same rhyme!
Perhaps some foolish idea wisdom must rout
or reflecting to see what insight is all about.
On such and such only a bit I thought I knew
and the lines would only be a few.
The magnificence of "To Half Dome via the Mist Trail" was leaven
enough that the pages went on to seven.

Try describing 30 objects on a stage
and only writing a single page.
Certain things of God require timely reflection.
To such God will give adequate recompense or special remuneration.
For years penning has been my role.
God will decide when each book is full.
Reflecting and musing is my part.
God does surely to thus impart.

Perhaps a pastor comes along with points of three
that do topically agree.
To further reflect I was very glad
as God did furthermore and enlighten and add.
The philosopher Christians shall be blest
because they need only do a little and God does the rest.
My meditation of the Word gets great gain
without any pain!
"No pain, no gain," has great repute.
Herein is an exception by which I may refute.
For satisfaction and accomplishment, you can later greatly rave
if you are a Christian surfer riding God's wave.
It is not just a decision between the foolish and the brave.
He who followed not God will be the knave.
Pick some spiritual thoughts and "ride the train."
See thereby what God shall cause you to gain.
Now of a two-word title I thought I could just pen lines of few.
I guess "Paucis Verbis" thereby went askew.

(paucis verbis [Latin]: in a few words.)

Audentes Fortuna Juvat
February 8, 1992

What do you think can be told
of fortune and daring by the time you get old?
Certainly, some will say they seemed to have a rule
to stay conservative and always play it cool.
Others were too foolish and went bankrupt or bust
or slightly better in that only investments turned to dust.
Still others concoct for their do-nothing life some justification.
They did nothing that could be called speculation.
Some merely saved money and put it in the bank.
Only with other savers they could rank.
Quite a few buy property for speculation.
After two years they match the saver's life accumulation.

Owning a building or land can be bad.
Buying when prices or interest was too high later makes one sad.
To great debt they can be bound.
It may be twenty years before they can turn things around.
Some do-nothings will say it was far more luck than skillful speculation.
They would not admit success was opportunity met with preparation.
Consider the parable of the talents.
The lord gave five, two, and one talent to three servants.
Two took them to the traders and they did much gain.
One hid his in the ground; only that much did remain.
His talent was given to the one who had ten.
The unprofitable servant would be cast into outer darkness then.
With your money you dare not be idle.
We are not to have time and money just to pleasantly while.
So, consider your whole financial situation and state
and employ all wisdom that you may profit before it is too late.

(audentes fortuna juvat [Latin] : fortune favors the bold)

Ex Pede Herculem
February 9, 1992

Is not looking at one's foot
like guessing the size of a tree when only seeing a root?
Or likewise from an omen or sign
one does try to construct a whole or do a further design.
A detective takes clues and in time
does therewith reconstruct the crime.
Thus what others see
is more than just show by a great degree.
Surely by logic you did infer
what from a symptom would happen or occur.
Many males have said, "Surely you take too much care
to judge me by long hair."
It is only natural to see something of the outside
and make conclusions about the inside.
If a house on the outside is very rundown,
one naturally conjectures that the inside would cause a frown.
So a thinker can be labeled a controversialist
just because wisdom requires one to be a rationalist.

Thus, a large foot is a declaration,
one's habits and appearance become a natural attestation.
Then in many things we need to pause.
What talk or rankling will this cause?

The Christian life is to be one of sanctification.
To a better testimony one is to make a progression.
Signs and omens.
Thereby discussions and conclusions!
Mien, appearance, countenance, air, looks, and demeanor.
Thereby opinions, speculations, and a thinker.
What you exhibit or show has an important role.
Like it or not – from a part we may judge of the whole.

(ex pede Herculem [Latin]: from the foot (we may judge the size of)
Hercules: from a part we may judge of the whole.)

Experto Credite
February 9, 1992

For some useless are books
and only of importance are things' looks.
Why was wisdom written?
For the fool it is a thing to be smitten.
Some run to foolishness like running off a cliff.
Many always a fool until they are laid stiff.
Some day you will lament.
Words of wisdom and experience are wise bestowment.
Why do you think some are exhorting
or from experience giving words of warning?
Most well-off speculators studied others of success.
Some fools think bothering to do such is dumbness.
Would you rather have success and think wisdom is something to admire
or would you more likely jump out of the frying pan into the fire?
The path of success should be the one on which to embark
or you will you needlessly shoot wide of the mark.
One could say, "Flirtation is not a thing to begin.
It could easily engulf you in a ruinous sin."
In reply, "All I want is a distraction for an hour or two."
Later, "My, oh my, I never thought this is what I would do."
It was just something you had to try
and there was no catcher in the rye.
Wisely listen to others who have run up against the wall
or of others who took a great fall.
Do you not realize that those who have been hurt
can now give great comfort?
Most often wisdom's best source
is from them who have run the course.
You can't cram too much into your head.
In pondering all actions of others, you will be wisely fed.

The mistakes of others let not evil assert,
but wisely be a thing to avert.
We ever need to be on guard to avoid errors and dumbness.
To Christlikeness via insight, wisdom, an experience we are to progress.

(experto credite [Latin]: believe one who has had experience)

Littera Scripta Manet
February 9, 1992

Many an inane fool
did get to rule.
Every king upon high
did go by and by.
Ponce de Leon could not find his fountain.
Eternal life shall ever be an insurmountable mountain.
You would be better off to think why
we live and why we die.
Thus, sure destruction of the body external.
What if there would be an inner life that would be eternal?
It has been said
and by scripture it has been read.
Consider this fact
and all it says and could exact.
Is it not declared, "The spirit is eternal, but the body will die?"
Consider also the rainbow of the sky.
If you think such beauty comes by itself,
your common sense is gone and you are "besides" yourself.
If you think the aurora borealis comes purely by chance,
methinks your brain got poked by some lance.
Fear of the eternal and thoughts of the highest may extract a cure.
Great wisdom shall come by thinking of all that does endure.
Who hung the millions of stars in the sky?
Is it something a learned human could try?
If it was by chance and evolutionary knowhow,
the earth should have had 12 moons by now.
Why no more evolving of new stars and lights?
Why no more coming about of spectacular new sights?
Thus, one needs to have more zeal
for what does last and is real.
Consider now what you should have already heard.
Study the history of God's chosen people and the Bible – God's Word.

(littera scripta monet [Latin]: the written letter abides.)

Quos Deus Vult Perdere Prius Dementat

February 15, 1992

The whole story I could not tell.
I know the "House of Usher" fell.
The story would be good to read
in that from therewith would be some lessons to heed.
With strange powers many do toy.
Know that the lure of such is an evil ploy.
Incense in a censer did Nadab and Abihu desire.
Fatal therein was their toying with strange fire.

The attractions of the New Age
are to some more than a passing rage.
How can some see Satan worship as profitable?
Death and destruction thereby are inevitable.
The lure of sin for a season
is about the only good reason.
Have you not heard you should weigh your gain
by any future loss or coming pain?
Though you step forward be one you adore,
what of the consequence of thereafter stepping back four?
We shall woefully continue to see fools rush in
without contemplation of anything later to chagrin.
Any later promises we can decry,
almost every one is an evil lie.
"Ten thousand souls in hell shall be yours to command!"
In darkness and fire, you shall put not your feet on any land.
You will not even have a fool's throne.
You will wish you had further studied the unknown.
In evil ranks the worshippers must go higher
or the sequel must tragically end the rules do require.
Most beyond age 25 do not last.
Pity your prime has not yet passed.
As the rules of the game were prearranged,
many became mentally deranged.
From thence come many raving lunatics.
Probably the greatest source of the clinical maniacs.
So, the story of many young people is very sad.
Before their destruction they are driven mad!
Let the facts and results be appalling.
All who enter the House of Usher will be in its falling.

(quos deus vult perdere prius dementat [Latin]: those whom a god
wished to destroy he first drives mad.)

Per Angusta Ad Augusta

February 15, 1992

Troubles we wish to alleviate.
From the path of adversity all would like to deviate.
But surely facts shall decree
that from evil you can't escape or flee.
The world of mirth
has one third of heaven turned evil and flung to earth.
Good angels also do here abide.
They are also by our side.
The omnipresent God is also at hand.
He stands before each angel and is in command.
Since the times of old
God's people were refined like gold.
Purity and Christlikeness is God's desire.
The dross can only be removed by some heat and fire.
Affliction and sorrow are appointed by the divine source.
The triune God has full control over our course.

So why are some saved at the 11th hour
and others like Job undergo trials that devour?
It is appointed!
Be one a king or Aaronic priest anointed.
All has a divine plot.
Things to us seem to fall by "lot."
It was not I who chose
the moment my soul from nothingness arose.
It is not I who can see or count every valence electron.
God will determine beforehand the outcome of every election.
Be you a Christian or one devouring with the sword,
every deed shall earn a punishment or reward.
Thus, our trials and pain
are for what we shall gain.
Our reproaches and afflictions will have great recompense.
In our trials we sometimes feel only madness and see nonsense.
Thought you not, "If this is for reward for a later day,
I would much rather go another way."

Others may see you for years
and have no idea of your enduring pain or many tears.
Then later you will be lifted on high.
Only then may you see some reasons why.
Other rewards are for eternity
and it will not be revealed until we get to glory.
To whatever position I have risen,
it will be because I have been chosen.

It is quite normal that people make comparisons.
We see before others' houses and provisions.
To see some of wealth you may say, "God's pet."
You know nothing I would surely bet.
To do a further probe
most would turn down the final wealth of Job.
Before you covet another's property and fine dishes,
You better think twice before you ask God for your wishes.

(per angusta ad augusta [Latin]: through difficulties to honors.)

Parturiunt Montes, Nascetur Ridiculus Mus
February 15, 1992

Oh, the world is in such pain.
Ye who labor, what do you gain?
There be many that work for peace
and shall continue until every war does cease.
Can we save more from misery
and raise all above poverty?
A fact we can't deny
is that many do surely, fervently try.
Now here and there
are accomplishments to declare.
Others look to some scapegoat to name
because a lot of things are the same.
Pharmacology now and then finds a cure or a better pill,
but morality seems steadily going downhill.
Many to find a lust or thrill
find it necessary to rape and kill.
Murder goes from once or twice
to a dozen times thrice.
Many lawbreakers upon their supposed "judgment day"
manage to get off free and then surely "crime does pay."

So you laborers ponder your chore.
The regression of nations and humanity is one to deplore.
Consider the labor that for little or naught was to gain.
You surely toil in vain.
"The poor will be with you always."
Effort to help others shall be good in many ways.
Consider what is part of God's plan.
What is in store for the wicked man?
Many do labor, toil, and plod
along without asking anything of God.

Can you remedy or change the course
of wicked mankind influenced by Satan's force?
Learn what can be done well for humanity.
Know that the idea of a cure all is sheer vanity.
The direction and your efforts in the daylight
need to be properly guided by prayer the previous night.
In much you will have no delight
as many things without God come to plight.
You without God need to reorder you house.
You are like "The mountains are in labor, and will only bring forth a ridiculous mouse."

(parturient montes, nascetur ridiculus mus [Latin]: the mountains
are in labor and a ridiculous mouse will be brought forth.)

Esse Quam Videri – I
September 7, 1992

I think that many do accordingly fare
as to the amount of preciseness that they therein take care.
Those who too often greatly and hazardly guess
too often wind up in a real mess.
Being accurate is a good habit,
but not to nit-pick until you have a fit.
Some things we want to be precise.
Other things are not critical, it would just be nice.
It would be impossible to have everything exact and absolute.
Decide what must be and in that be resolute.

Most important is how we shall spend eternity.
Through Jesus and the Word it comes to us as a simplicity.
Some hold eternal life to be a lucky conjecture.
They hope, but are not really sure.
The Word promises us that we may surely know.
The Spirit of God attests that it is so.
Too many today can only guess.
You shall be beyond a tragic mess.

Of salvation all can surely know.
Then as disciples we are to spiritually grow.
Salvation is not just a know-how.
Jesus wants to live through us now.
The Word must we carefully divide.
Too many for accuracy shoot very wide.
We must carefully study to know what the Word does mean.
Not good enough is, "thus and thus it does seem."

Many things of the triune God are revealed.
Some things shall to humans remain concealed.
Most realize that they can make the best of a situation,
especially if by facts and knowledge they make a decision.
Proverbs exhorts us to instruction to make us wise.
Learning the fool does despise.
Instruction, reproof, and correction are necessary for the wise man.
The fool avoids it all he can.

"These things have I written unto you…that ye may know…"
Surely a superior position to, "I think so."
Best not to guess what will be.
"Know" that before Christ everyone shall bow his knee.
List all things important, one by one.
Be assured of each and you will have well begun.
There is much that can't be left to chance you should deem.
Certainty is a thing to be rather than to seem.

(esse quam videri [Latin]: to be rather than to seem)

Esse Quam Videri – II
September 7, 1992

Know that everyone who is Christ's disciple
is to go forth as a good example.
Only the power within us
can cause us to be properly thus.
In godly living most wish to abide.
Know that Satan will attack your weakest side.
He can simply find you out,
without a doubt.
Think not that you are above his power.
With God's permission he can shame you within an hour.
Let not pride make you feel so grand and tall.
You will be shortly due for a great fall.
A good testimony is not just a matter of good impromptu
nor can anyone give you a sure menu.
It can be something you work on for years
and in a few moments being remiss can put you in tears.
God must keep us going forward
else Satan causes us to be froward.
One's walk may appear to be good or so seem,
but man does so easily incorrectly deem.
For more prayer we need a greater zest.
This only will put us at our best.

For Christianity to peak,
we need call on God to speak.
All nature must obey God's voice or will.
Remember Jesus and the sea, "Peace, be still."
Judging myself would put me on the spot.
Merely to seem I would rather not.
Our virtue by our own might attains only a faint gleam.
Better by God's power to be rather than seem.

Facillis Descensus Averno
September 8, 1992

Life does come and so quickly does go.
Very brief, everyone should surely know.
About the thereafter most really just guess.
Meditation of eternity causes most much stress.
Too many are preoccupied upon how they should live
and what they need to earn, pay, or give.
Death is a guaranteed occurrence.
Over such all have a need to gain assurance.
All have their appointed hour
and need to contemplate the effects of a higher power.

One's wishes and hopes are a useless role
when found there is a higher being that has control.
To simply live and die is to one's natural state
shall surely lead to one's fate.
God can't be denied.
Only a trite bit of logic need be applied.
Are not evil, Satan, and demons ever before our face?
Is not wickedness seeming to consume most of the human race?
Are not most people ending up going in a Godless way?
Many do sadly depart each day.

Jesus said, "No man cometh unto the Father but by me."
This is an inescapable decree.
Salvation is for those that believe.
Jesus must we also accept and receive.
Not to obey has one great cost.
You shall forever be eternally lost.
Christianity and "salvation" are things most people ignore.
Perhaps to consider such is too great a chore.
So easy is it then to get on the road to destruction.
To avoid it all must heed the Word's instruction.
Accept Christ – much more difficult (?), but necessary.

Ignore Christ – the road to evil is easy.

(facillis descensus averno [Latin]: the descent to Avernus is easy:
The road to evil is easy)

Fas Est Et Ab Hoste Doceri
September 9, 1992

Does not scripture speak of the roaring lion, our enemy?
Have you not also heard, "Know thine adversary?"
All defeated in war
can from the adversary learn more.
Scripture does take great care
to warn us of our present spiritual warfare.
The enemy is about us as a great flood.
We wrestle not against flesh and blood.
About the warfare there is much to read and tell.
Only by greater knowledge will one fare well.
The Christian warriors are to learn of their foes.
The unlearned shall undergo many woes.
We are to put on the armor of God that we may stand.
Be wholly armed any warfare would demand.

We are to take the helmet of salvation.
The sword of the Spirit is to be a companion.
We are to utilize much prayer and supplication.
For the warfare each saint needs much preparation.
The enemy is not easy to beat.
We need to learn from every defeat.
Fighting Satan is not cops and robbers with some fine toys.
You will go down like Ma Barker and her boys.
Entreat God much as there is much to learn
and many things we need to correctly discern.
The Word we need to dutifully heed.
The Lord will provide us with all we need.
In battles we can bring the enemy to a stop.
Learning much knowledge will put us on top.

(fas est et ab hoste doceri {Latin}: it is right to learn from
an enemy.)

Nil Sine Numine
September 10, 1992

Oh, world gone awry.
To fix, many do earnestly try.
Of evil there is an endless supply.
To reason and sanity little seems to comply.
Society and order seem to daily regress.
The fixers can't really seem to make any real progress.
Many of us Christians are very sad.
The economy and morality have gone mad.
A near bankrupt congress has robbed future generations.
For a massive debt you can't make reparations.
Evil and chaos seem to reign.
We see daily ever more crime and pain.
A list of woes does not desist.
In what then is one's sanity to consist?
Now near the edge of economic survival.
Oh, how the world needs a revival.
Many tyrants madly shake their rod.
We Christians have refuge only in God.
He only sits on the Sides of the North throne.
The Savior has made himself known.
We underwent judgement for much sin.
So went all history again and again.
No one comes to power
unless it is God's appointed hour.
Nothing is merely putting humanly forth what is good.
Many have done all they could.
Yea, indeed, wickedness has greatly abounded.
Restorers of righteousness are dismayed and confounded.
Oh, world, you are seemingly at the end of your rope.
Only in God can we have any hope.
Only in prayer in my heart can I say, "Peace, be still."
Nothing without the divine will.

(nil sine numine [Latin]: nothing without the divine will.)

Qui Separabit?
September 11, 1992

Surely there are many who look to eternity
and have no assurance of eternal security.
We need to believe that all who are redeemed are secure in Christ forever.

You will surely think awry if on human logic you endeavor.
That one can have salvation and lose it is too often heard
because some read not or believe not God's Word.
Those in doubt
need to get into the Word to check it out.
The redeemed are a matter of the Father's giving.
"…that of all that He hath given me I should lose nothing."
If you believe in Jesus, upon an everlasting life you may rely.
Jesus said it, can He lie?
The sheep of Jesus does He cherish.
"I give unto them eternal life; and they shall never perish,
neither shall any pluck them out of my hand."
One greater than God it would surely demand.
"My Father, who gave them to me, is greater than all."
Believe this as truth or God's Word is to you a story quite tall.
"No one is able to pluck them out of my Father's hand."
Again, I say that a greater power would have to take command.
Not believing this is matter of the Word to you refused.
Read all scripture and believe that you be the less confused.
Confusion is surely within Satan's power.
It will be dispelled by reading the Word many an hour.
"To those in Christ Jesus there is no condemnation."
Believe God and eternal security will give you no consternation.
Upon the greatest power does one's assurance go accordingly thus.
Who shall separate us?

(que separabit [Latin]: Who shall separate us?)

(Eternal security: John 6:37-40, 10:27-30, Romans 8:1,38,39;
I Cor. 1:4-8; I Peter 1:5)

Veni, Vidi, Vici
September 11, 1992

Veni, vidi, vici, for so many a thing to do.
Veni, vidi, vici, did you?
For some a great statement and promise.
Upon what ground do you base your premise?
Perhaps you are a great conquistador.
Did you thoroughly evaluate what you did conquer?
Perhaps you wanted to conquer from your youth.
Did you really ferret out the truth?
All power, possessions, and life shall one day flee.
What then when from the body you are free?
Did you consider when possessions and the body do remain

what would happen in your new domain?
Did you also conquer this domain's throne
or perchance could you stand all alone?
Do you think you will be the captain at the helm
of this new realm?
Can your mind also conquer eternity
or does it remain in total obscurity?
Perhaps you can wear a country like a weapon on your hip,
but upon the thereafter can you get a likewise grip?
A penny today is not as good as $1000 tomorrow.
A forfeiture of tomorrow could bring about great sorrow.
Did you weigh well whether death ushers in a great flight
or whether you will come about to a miserable plight?
Are you wise in your own conceit?
You are more than likely a victim of Satan's deceit.
Many kings had kingdoms very large and whole.
What would it profit if you would then lose your soul?
Your soul is a better thing than a kingdom to advance.
Who but a fool would dare to take a great chance?
For many conquering was life's ultimate truth and story.
I will see if your premise was on God's promise if I see you in glory.

(veni, vidi, vici [Latin]" I came, I saw, I conquered.)

Pereunt et Imputantur
September 14, 1992

Life going on day by day.
Often almost all toil and no play.
Evil are the days.
Mostly for taxes, shelter, and bills one pays.
So necessary that the kingdom of God does advance.
Do nothing and evil gains with an almost 100% chance.
That a good steward tithes or gives is more than mere advice.
In these inflationary days it is more so of a sacrifice.
One calculates and spins much around in his head.
Toiling much many don't seem to be going ahead.
Thus one needs now and then pause.
I am advancing whose cause?
In a merry-go-round race one becomes easily confounded.
The fruits of the storehouse have not abounded.
Time does surely go on by.
In that one need not even try.
For all of the toil I have pained,
has my earthly kingdom really gained?

So easy in some ways to see the growth of one's treasure.
How about that which has an invisible measure?
As invisible as the soul.
To God it plays an all-important role.
How easily man beholds an oak or redwood tree.
This invisible thing God does easily, visibly see.
Man enters debits and credits in a ledger book.
Upon man's spiritual state God does similarly look.
We accumulate wealth that all can visibly admire.
Do you know our invisible and visible deeds shall be tested by fire?
Some thing will cause loss and others produce gain.
After the fire how much shall remain?

In spiritual things only God can lead and a purpose instill.
Time slowly ripples on by like a rill.
Too late for many a truth shall be made plain.
To fill the wrong barn many will too laboriously pain.
Satan has come to deceive, destroy, cheat, and even just gyp.
Lord, upon my spiritual state give me an insightful grip.
For Thy kingdom's advance, help me to progress.
Left alone all shall surely regress.
One has no abundance of days to idly waste.
The point of reckoning surely makes haste.
For most the judgment day will too quickly occur.
Pereunt et Imputantur.
(Pereunt et Imputantur [L]: the hours pass away and are reckoned to our account)

Ob Scurum Per Obscurious
September 17, 1992

Scholars running around left and right.
A lot of people getting more uptight.
People need no longer guess
whether most everything is a mess.
A congress trying to spend their way to prosperity.
Rapidly enveloping all in economic misery.
On solutions you should be bent.
I see only chaos as a result of all the money that was spent.
Truly you are wrapped in the paralysis
of analysis.
All is visibly going backwards.
No help from all the brains of the scholars and nerds.
In your futile struggles have you become quite inured?
Hah, Washington wizards, the answers are to you entirely obscured.
"The president is not doing enough!"

That came from a mind capable of only dumb stuff.
The economy is comprised of $4.5 trillion gnp.
The "economy" is all money spent you should agree.
Poor leadership all of the liberals chime.
You put him where he can't add or take away one budgetary dime.
He controls $5 trillion as much as the man on the moon.
Someone is a liar, blinded, or as crazy as a loon.
Any common-sense ideas you wanted not.
You thought by the election you could put him on the spot.
To the enlightened it should be no surprise
that God the Father controls the scales before your eyes.
I see this entire land loaded with sin.
Unless changed no new prosperity may begin.

I hear many solutionless solutions being resounded.
No doubt your confusion is twice confounded.
To stall a recovery many have deliberately been a louse.
It seemed worth sacrificing the economy to win the White House.
Allegiance to the golden rule you have none.
Only the ungodly would sacrifice people so a position could be won.
To explain things without God's insightful light
will ensure everyone's doomful plight.
Worthless will be the paths on which you embark.
You are as good as a bunch of people running around in the dark.
The power of our doomful state is hidden from your eyes.
That it is not even human would be to you a total surprise.
Not resolving the problem may put you in a fit.
You can't even put your finger on it.
A knowledge of God and Christ the situation does demand.
The control of all is in the Father's hand.
The whole thing to the unredeemed is quite obscure.
The Jesus I serve is to you even more obscure.

(ob scurum per obscurious [L]: explaining the obscure my the more obscure.)

Multim in Parvo
September 18, 1992

Many look at all of their goods in hand
and to get much more is always in demand.
"Be satisfied" is quite easy to give as advice.
All recognize that most often more would be nice.
It is of necessity we oft take our eyes off the physical
to concentrate on the spiritual.
Too many are madly chasing dreams and success.

In a few important ways much does regress.
For most success comes by neither toil or hocus pocus.
You need to ask God to change your focus.
Religion is to too many a deviant.
We redeemed find happiness in following Christ the servant.
Spiritual gifts were given to serve.
Too many are keeping them in reserve.
Many little things are accomplished one by one.
This is how much of the Lord's work is done.
Thus, the servant's role
is one God does greatly extol.
It is what God did devise.
He who follows Jesus will be very wise.
To be a power broker or king
is usually the only worldly one's thing.
In the lust for too much your world usually falls apart.
By Christ you have a need for some instruction to impart.
Though for some the idea of a servant is a role that would belittle.
Yea, but the saints in Christ know the richness of much in little.

(multum in parvo [L]: much in little)

Cadit Quaestio
October 29, 1992

You who would strongly aver a theory or promise,
are you sure of the necessary premise?
A seeming sound theory is only a speculation
without the proper foundation.
Certainly it should be logical that every dissertation
can't be based solely on human rationalization.
I could have a verity that I would greatly hold dear,
but upon a baseless premise I would be a sounding chanticleer.
I extol all that in every forth put verity
know that it is well built on a certainty.

Consider also when a certain debate and contention
revolves around a certain question.
A certain question is asked.
Then support thereto by logic and facts is greatly tasked.
The postulate exudes much deduction.
The reasoner well states everything with a good explanation.
An arguer often comes forth with such a flair
that his charisma of persuasion usually pervades the air.
As the negative or opposer you will often lament

because the affirmative knows how to put things in cement.
Though the debater seems to get the upper hand,
a greater scope of discussion may be in demand.

The logician's arguments may be one-sided.
The conclusions were thereby incorrectly decided.
One may have been wise in his own conceit.
He could easily become a victim of evil deceit.
That there was not a greater question you did thereon prey.
Your question drops and the argument collapses I say.
Some enhance material possessions as security.
It is extolled at least somewhat by the majority.
It often becomes difficult to say how much "stuff"
it takes to accumulate to be enough.
Too little is something to deplore.
Security is directly related to getting more.
Security is big houses, a yacht, and much money in the bank.
Thereby many do rate their rank.
Full security does demand
that you have a lot of goods in hand.
Security is debated and measured by "how much."
I suggest many discussions do go as such.
Your money and possessions will all be taken away one day.
The question drops and the argument collapses I say.
(cadit quaestio [L]: the question drops: the argument collapses)

Splendide Mendax
November 5, 1992

"You make a poor liar," you may have heard.
Some pretenses are so obvious it is almost absurd.
Such will occur by the amateur and fool
you would note as a general rule.
Such a start for boys and girls from the country and city.
Thus, they begin an apprenticeship to deception, a pity.
Though good in your drama, life will end a Greek tragedy.
You will rue you had not lived for Christ and honesty.

The learner becomes good at fronting a sham.
Discovery of truth not easy unless given a careful exam.
Lie a little now and then later most of the time.
You are being entrapped in a life of crime.
Instilling confidence into your victims is a must.
The sucker thinks you are one he can surely trust.
Some become con men with great talent and flair.

Then some vanish as if into thin air.
"He sure put up a good front."
For such some victim will bear calamity's brunt.

There are yet two higher levels.
The incarnated experts and the devils.
Some real experts are also very wise in their own conceit.
You are a victim of Satan's deceit.
Many are influenced by evil power.
They can outwit most in any given hour.
Many people are naturally quite glib
and can very adeptly ad lib.
Evil angels play an important role.
As one lusts for more, evil gets more control.
A blind aura of trustworthiness sets a snare.
So beware.
By people and angels there is much deception.
Evil can empower the delusion.
Satan works with trickery, cunning and guile.
Many learn from him and deceive with a noble style.

Though to persuasion you may be resistant,
the deceiver is usually amazingly persistent.
Now consider the amazing logic of the lie.
Quite well cloaked the falsehood that does underlie.
A person as sincere as the day is long.
One could hardly go wrong.
So are the lies Satan has us confront.
Totally dissipated when you get the sham's brunt.
A feeling beforehand instilled as a southern gentleman
keeping his word with every effort put forth that he can.
Promises of a nobleman, earl, or knight.
Dealing with one of such "integrity" is a delight.
The lie is manifested when your "ship coming in" hits the rocks.
A display of integrity at its best, but splendide Mendax.

(splendide mendax [L]: nobly untruthful)

Quot Homines, Tot Sententiae
November 7, 1992

Ideas and solutions do flourish and abound.
So many to be found.
Get in a crowd and you will find out
if you discuss politics, without a doubt.

So many to discuss our national plight.
Try to guess who is wrong and who is right.
Many insist everything is the president's fault.
He is a good one to assault.
"If only he would be a better leader."
So the hunt begins for a better commander.
What do you know?
Everyone is a disappointment as time does go!
The thrust of the political debate.
How do we turn this country into a near perfect state?
We know that for years our present congress was a victim of paralysis
of analysis.
Deficit spending to get the economy on track.
I saw more things losing ground and more falling back.
During campaigning there were many charges and insults.
Afterwards the critics examining the results.
The concept of good vs. evil did no one face.
(As if God was out lost in space.)
In that, each analyzer was a totally ignorant fool.
God indeed causes every king to fall or rule.

Oh you agnostics and atheists, to your surprise
there is a God that can bless or bring about everyone's demise.
The real situation most do not at all confront.
The concepts of God, Satan, good, and evil should be forefront.
By a good king righteousness may have a hurrah.
An evil king will help lead a land to doom like Sodom and Gomorrah.
Of utmost importance analyze a country's spiritual state.
That the majority are seeking or shunning God should center your debate.
Repel God and He becomes your destructor.
Repent and Jesus Christ will be the leader
that all do presently seek.
Only obedience to God makes blessings peak.
Expressing opinions causes tempers to flair and boil.
Such will be of people who deny God as absolute and royal.
A thousand people and a thousand solutions.
Yea, and ten times as many resolutions.
There is truth through only One.
Only by God will the battle over evil be won.
Answers and truth will be found
when in prayer and the Word the saints abound.
Today too few pray and too many accost.
This country is indeed mostly a people that are lost.
Wickedness does more and more abound.
Only hope through God can be found.

(quot homines, tot sententiae [L]: there are as many opinions as there are men.)

Vexilla Regis Prodeunt
December 6, 1992

Afore 500 years John Skelton wrote
about our Savior who was smote.
"The King's banner on the field is splayed, (middle English)
the cross's mystery can't be nayed.
Tis no small thing
that Christ can become our personal King.

Walk you about as if His banner is high?
Know you not that the Lord is always nigh?
Consider it emblematically visible and invisible.
Now a tad of discussion to make this symbol divisible.
Such an illustration not in average knowledge's ken,
Something is displayed by all women and men.
Once saved something no one can cast aside.
A Holy Spirit to begin an eternal life now inside.
When your spirit steps out of the body a delight
to see all saints emit God's light.
God within a vessel or room has a presence that can't be hidden.
A thing Satan can't disburden.

Many are seen as Christ's, no doubt
because they openly show Christ wherever they go about.
Twill never be their will
that of the gospel message they be a long while still.
Ye, who are Christ's, emit you always a favorable light?
I speak of behavior an aura perceived by all in sight.
The God within and without surely invisible.
Though surely as you walk some perception quite visible.
Can others well perceive an invisible loving light?
An invisible emittance beheld by the mind's sight.
I suggest that some without task
display a love and joy that others to want to therein bask.
To speak of Christ some Christians would be better if they did not try.
The cause of Christ they seem to only decry.
O Christian, take heed of your every manner.
How well flies about you Christ's banner?

(vexilla regis prodeunt [L]: The King's banners are displayed.)

Corruptio Optimi Pessima
February 17, 1992

Surely one can see it a terrible plight
when the reputations of the best are put to flight.
The prize of Satan's war
is cutting into the church's core.
Paul wrote that an elder must be above reproach.
Assumingly corruption was to never encroach.
It should be the goal of all to have an honorable reputation.
None are to love or tolerate corruption.
Enhancement of character and soul
should be the normal Christian goal.
Even when a politician's top aide falls from grace
he can bring to his boss great disgrace.
Corruption in the president's cabinet
sets him back a bit you can surely bet.
Then it will only naturally cause more speculation
of how much there is of undiscovered corruption.
Is not keeping your word synonymous with your character?
Quite unrespectable is a promise breaker.
From movies and times of old have you not heard
that nothing was more important than a southerner keeping his word?

The church can't have reputation or fame
for the Lord unless no one can lay blame.
The leaders are to be models and examples.
Can corruption produce good disciples?
For examples it is not too hard to search
to see where sin quite well destroyed a church.
Many followers are greatly shaken
when one out of the top or ranks for sin is taken.
For a shining example you will utterly fail
if a crime just about lands you in jail.
Know that many years of effort, work, fruitful labor, and resolve
can in a single stroke of action all dissolve.
Elevated Christians or church leaders are Satan's favorite prey.
Hurting Christ through them gives him a real heyday.
So, for all, in everything think twice before you do
so that it ends not in an act to rue.
Climbing the ladder to wealth or fame may be neat,
but Satan will surely try to kick the ladder out from under your feet.
Labor endlessly to hold your good name.
In this spiritual war it is the enemy's prize game.

(corruptio optimi pessima [L]: the corruption of the best is the worst of all.)

Unity in the Camp
December 28, 1990

Know ye the troop is in a war?
Because of their unity many victories they will score.
There is unity from the general all the way down.
To swerve from the cause none dares wince or frown.
They need have no disciplinary sessions.
Take heed for some valuable lessons.

They know well it is a spiritual fight.
They never rest or take time for delight.
None would think to waive or pause
from carrying out their mission and cause.
You should guess or know
that each tediously studies his foe.
Each trooper knows the rules and regulations.
There can be no deviations.

Study would show they are a dedicated team.
Far more unified than most armies it would seem.
To carry out the mission is a burning desire.
Such resoluteness one certainly must admire.
They have no quitters or AWOL's you should know.
Only forward with victory mindedness they go.
Any general would be proud and could beam
as he looked out and saw that such was his team.

If you think the above describes the church or humanity,
you have lost your sanity.
The descriptions were accurate and right on course.
It describes Satan and his force.
They do not waiver or pause
from giving 100% to carry on their cause.

The Christian army shoots their wounded it is known.
Many are by every wind of false doctrine easily blown.
The Christian army is a divisive lot.
It is easy for the enemy to plot.
A new recruitment will probably be disciplined you can bet,
if he doesn't toe the line like a seasoned vet.
They will fight over the color of a nursery.

Upon their own kind they inflict a lot of misery.
At times disciplinary action needs to be taken,
but over immediate "sanctification by the Spirit" many are mistaken.
Divide and conquer seems to be a profitable strategy.
Not too difficult to conquer when an army lacks harmony.
Know thine adversary it is said.
Christ the King is above all you have read.
Unity in the camp is a necessity.
To arms, report for duty!

The Dark Side of the Force
March 25, 1991

Know of the forces in the air.
They enhance an ability to a flair.
Do you wonder how you get so fired up with wrath?
The dark side will pave you a quick path.
Does it seem someone pushed a hot button?
Tis all mental where it is done.
You will eventually find
the forces read and influence your mind.
To the Word, to arms, humans beware!
The force encroached all it may dare.
The dragon and one third were all hurled out.
The force is sure, without a doubt.

The evil emperor confronted the Jedi face to face.
Each for power had his presumed base.
Evil to the core.
The dark side did the Jedi abhor.
"Come forth with your might.
Slay me if it be your delight.
I can see hatred in your eyes.
Indignation and fury are on the rise.
You feel you must conquer me out of your righteous pride.
It will not be long until I win you to my side."

Certain injustices we must correct.
To careful discernment we must be subject.
Anger, envy, and hatred can steam and boil.
They pass not the most regal or royal.
By such evil hopes to consume you right to the soul.
Total domination is their goal.
Know and feel the force.
They can easily suck the unwary down a destructive course.

Evil is constantly by your side.
It wishes to be to you as a bride.
At your weak point they will whittle.
You are next to them small, weak, and little.

Think twice before hatred lures you down its path.
A consuming fire is a vengeful wrath.
"Vengeance is mine," saith the Lord.
Is He incapable of rendering due reward?
No evil shall be forgotten any day.
"I shall repay."
Call unto the Lord to keep you in the light.
Discernment of action needs to be constantly in sight.
Pray for guidance of your action's course.
Beware the dark side of the force!

Spiritual Warfare: Tactics of the Enemy
June 2, 1991

Jesus called our enemy the "father of lies."
Lies are keys to Satan's success it should be no surprise.
We should not choose the path of least resistance.
It is not consistent to Christians and obedience.
If you are in Christ's fold,
you can't succumb to Satan's mold.
God has equipped us to fight him we see in the Word.
Know thine adversary you have also heard.
Satan wants us to be ignorant of his tactics and schemes.
Knowledge could blow apart his plots at the seams.
There are many things Satan does and tries.
Let us consider three of his lies.

He wants people to think he is not real. (1)
For many this thought has its appeal.
John 8:44 says Satan is a liar and the father of it.
Lies make a lot of his schemes succeed or fit.
We need to tell
others of the dangers of hell.
Have we prayed lately that Satan would be hindered?
Prayer can restrain him but neglect lets his plans be cindered.
Today there are many who say
we can all believe what we want and we will all be o.k.
Satan can get away with a lot if we believe he does not exist.
God lets us do much if we merely resist.

The second lie goes to the opposite extreme.
It is successful on some I deem.
He is too powerful for us to resist. (2)
There is therefore nothing we can do to make him cease and desist.
He is the opposite of God some think.
He is not – these people need rethink.
"Keep away from him and you will be ok."
But evil will never stay away from us a single day!
He was in Eden where there were many precious stones to admire.
He walked up and down in the midst of the stones of fire.
Satan was the real king of Tyre.
Of the earthly ruler he was in essence the sire.
All to the will of God do bow.
Satan is obedient to him even now.
He is not too powerful to defy.
He will never be the power on high.

Lie three is that we can approach him casually. (3)
Those who think thusly will fare miserably.
"If he is defeated, we need not worry about him."
Satan is not here to merely fulfill his every whim.
A wounded rat will fight with the courage of a lion most brave.
A fight to the death – not the mere whining of a knave.
The rat has nothing to lose.
Satan wants to consume or devour us, not just inflict a bruise.
Some think they can dabble with evil workings.
Like ants under elephants' feet for stamina testings.
So shall you fare.
Don't even dare!

Approach Satan from truth and light.
All else shall lead to a foolish plight.
Be mindful of his power.
He is a strong force able to devour.
Do not dabble in any darkness.
Dabbling in darkness and putting your hand in fire – a likeness.
Do not oppose him in your own strength.
He will beat you at any length.

Be prayerful in conflict.
Prayer and preparedness your life should depict.
In opposing Satan we must be forceful.
God has given us the power as believers to make our resistance meaningful.
We need to have knowledge.
We may be able to stand the devil with God's armor is the scriptural pledge.

Spiritual Warfare: Identities of the Enemy
June 30 – July 7, 1991

The effectiveness of Satan's schemes will not last
if we are aware of how he has acted in the past.
All need to watch, study, and take care.
Of Satan's plots and plans we must be aware.
We need to have a handle on the Word
to counter him or we'll be ineffective if it is seldom heard.
The Word needs to be hidden in our heart
that it would not depart.
We need to recall it in the heat of battle.
Our confidence will not be something Satan can easily rattle.
When we meditate,
we can find amazing power to cause evil's fate.
The Word is where we get answers.
It is the source from which victory occurs.
There are four identities Satan has assumed.
There are doubtless others by which people were consumed.
Though for roles he has more.
Let us now look at a particular four.

He was "The Deceiver" you should agree
from Genesis chapter three.
It is no surprise to find
that his target is your mind.
If he can get you to believe his lie,
he can render you ineffective for Christ by and by.
His weapon is lies.
Getting one to doubt God's Word is what he tries.
He questioned God's Word scripture does tell.
He made Eve to question it as well.
He denied that the Word was true.
Death could not be an actuality to rue.
Adam and Eve had not seen death so they
could only go on the Word day by day.
Satan offered them the chance to be
like God by eating from the tree.
This was also his own desire.
To be equal to God would give a position to admire.
His purpose is to make us ignorant (by his jives)
to the will of God for our lives.
When he can diminish the authority of the Word of God, it thus
has little practical value to us.
Being a victim because Satan played the deceiver,
we have all been a receiver.

Very little reasoning must one probe
to see Satan as "The Destroyer" in reading about Job.
His target is everything that you have.
When you feel like a poor beguiled knave,
you doubt the divine purpose of God.
Satan wants us to believe we are always under some cruel master's rod.
God can use it to
make us like Christ, not just time to rue.
Suffering can cause us to grow.
Our faith can come together or fall apart though.
Satan wants to make us impatient with God's will.
He would have us think we are always on a laborious treadmill.
God only builds our character through patient suffering.
There are no quick fixes or any type of instant building.
The grace of God sustains us through tough
times and keeps us going when things are really rough.
Paul's infirmity was not just an evil device.
To have it removed he pleaded thrice.
"My grace is sufficient for thee."
Paul learned to rely on the grace of God and not "me."

Although Satan often gets you by being a fooler,
his goal is to be "The Ruler."
One of king David's sins was in numbering the people.
To Levi and Benjamin, the king's word was abominable.
David's numbering the soldiers was to God a defiance.
The strength of the numbers would be a new reliance.
For God he then would have less of a need.
Satan's target is your will.
With his things he would like you to get your fill.
We can get into a battle of asserting
our will and making it the focus of our concentrating.
Satan appealed to David's pride
to make him independent of God in what he did decide.
Satan wants to convince people today
they are good enough on their own and in their own way.
Our defense is the indwelling Spirit.
We yield our will to make things spiritually fit.

Surely we know Satan is an evil infuser.
In Zechariah chapter 3 we see him as "The Accuser."
His target is our heart and conscience,
the awareness of the moral right and wrong in each deed and performance.
Joshua, the priest, had on dirty clothes to represent the people's sin.
Only through Jesus can we be cleansed and thus newly begin.
Satan's purpose is to get us to give up on ourselves and our resolve.
He would like to see our entire conscious fortitude dissolve.

Our defense is the interceding Son
of God and by Him the battle is won.
Yea, Satan is our accuser.
The One who redeemed us is greater.
We have a defense at every step of the battle.
Jesus will help us in our every struggle.

Spiritual Warfare: Footholds of the Enemy
July 21, 1991

When it comes to warfare, the apostle Paul laid it on the line.
He suggested some areas of our lives to examine
to be sure we are not giving the enemy a foothold.
Seven areas of vulnerability need be discussed and told.
Satan gets a powerful foothold when we allow sin to persist.
He takes every inch you cede – he can't resist.
He will use it to make us ineffective
for the Lord if we allow ourselves to be subjective.
We need to make a searching and fearless
moral inventory of ourselves or we will spiritually regress.
Paul warned the Ephesians (Ch. 4) of their need.
We can't give Satan ground for him to put in his seed.

Truthfulness is a necessity.
We are to allow no pretense, falsehood, or mendacity.
Do everything so everyone can see
an unvarnished authenticity.
A little lie
usually leads to a bigger lie.
You can give evil a place in your heart.
Let Satan enter and he will not soon depart.

Our temper can flair up but must desist.
Anger becomes sinful when we allow it to persist.
Anger is a common emotion
and often goes in motion.
We can go down a vengeful path
if we let the sun go down on our wrath.
Deep scars anger can leave.
Such a state the Spirit shall grieve.

Trustworthiness is an area that can be very widespread.
Outright stealing is not the only way which trustworthiness has fled.
A thief most people would abhor.
Paul wrote, "Let him that stole steal no more."

We can also rob when we work too much.
Yea, a form of thievery is as such.
We are not very good if we do not have a sympathetic ear.
Wanting too many toys leaves nothing for the Lord it does appear.
In Ezra we read the temple was neither built nor fused
when cedars for their own houses were used.
When we bury our talents the church body
gets no benefit or edification and they have no utility.
We need to be a giver
so others can benefit as a receiver.

Our tongue can easily be a source of corrupt communication.
We need to build others up and use it for edification.
If we concentrate on using it to meet other people's needs,
We will be less apt to use it for hurtful deeds.
Books written on the tongue will stack up many a yard.
It can be a little tyrant so we need to be constantly on guard.

Our integrity is a purity
of character and fundamental to our dignity.
We are not to cause God sorrow by the way we live.
Grieve not the Holy Spirit is good advice to give.
All like an elder of the church we should be.
No one is to be able to point a finger at our behavior or integrity.
To the Christian cause we can have no fidelity
if we do not maintain our integrity.
Without integrity our walk of faith will not be steadfast
and very few things that count will last.

Our tendencies are numerous you will see
if you think about them to any degree.
We are to get rid of spite and bitterness.
Concentrate on expressing kindness.
Angry flareups are the result of not containing rage.
These can grow and reach a dangerous stage.
Bitterness keeps track of a score of wrongs.
You will have little joy to manifest itself in gleeful songs.
We need to put away anger, slander, and evil speaking.
Put away angry shouting, noisy asserting, and clamor.
Malice and hateful feelings will find some outward way to recur.
The study of tendencies will easily fill a book.
We have one more character at which we need to look.

Our tenderness is an area we want to cultivate.
We need to be loving and compassionate.
It is an area in which we need to take stock.
A development of this Satan will surely try to block.

Tenderhearted in the original text was "good guts to one another."
Tenderness promotes good deeds to a sister or brother.
Since times of old
Satan has always tried to stop us cold.

There are many areas that God must search us
and cleanse us.
You may try all you can
but there is no such thing as "the self-made man."
In prayer we need to take inventory.
With the Lord's help we can have a "good Christian story."
There are too many areas to go awry and remain "at large."
The success story will come from letting God take charge.

Spiritual Warfare: Confronting the Enemy – The Belt of Truth
July 25, 1991

How can we stay oriented
in the midst of a culture filled
with lies, Satan's seed?
God has provided us with all the protection we need.
Each piece of armor is given by
God to counter-attack everything Satan does try.
Behind every sin there is a lie.
There is some irrationality that does belie.
"Cheating on your taxes will get you ahead."
Not so when the great judgment is all done and said.
Lie after lie will come about and occur.
The belt of truth is our first piece of armor.
Without armor many blows would be fatally felt.
We are responsible for girding the belt.
On aspects we will consider four.
There are doubtlessly more.

The person of truth is the Word.
The Word became flesh you have read and heard.
Jesus is this person.
Only by Him was our battle won.
Truth is not in a set of beliefs.
Mere tenets or isms provide no reliefs.
Apart from the person of truth nothing will do.
Satan will win every battle against you.
We know the truth because
we know him who is above all of our laws.
The relationship to Christ is foundational

to the belt of truth – indeed, very fundamental.

The <u>Word of Truth</u> exemplifies the Savior's sovereignty.
In it we find salvation and realize the de facto authority.
All things need to be subjected to the Word of the great "I am."
The light differentiates holy things from a base flim-flam.
Too many do what they feel is right.
The heart is wicked, the flesh carnal – guides to a sure plight.
Ancient Israel's wicked times were no surprise.
"Everyone did what was right in his own eyes."
The Bereans diligently searched the scriptures to see
if what Paul was saying was indeed scripture's decree.
When man's self-styled doctrine is illumined by the Word,
it oft quickly is seen as confused, inconsistent, senseless, or absurd.
A good study of the Word takes effort and is exacting.
Such endeavors will send a few false teachers quickly "a packing."
Pity for so many the Word is an object too dormant or sour.
You shall not partake of its experiential power.
You are askew if you think this should be a tizzy high.
Full awareness never goes thither but is always nigh.
Your study of the Word is God's delight.
He shall illumine your understanding by discerning light.

The <u>Spirit of Truth</u> gives us guidance.
He is the inner essence of discernment's radiance.
No one comes to God unless He draws us.
You have a following, leading, or guidance by thus.
The Spirit gives us a nudging
in the areas of Christian growth and maturing.
We are to test leadings against the Word.
Evil shall also be seen, felt, or heard.
Pray, "Lord, if this be of You, let the feelings grow stronger.
If it is evil, let me feel it no longer."
If a leading is seemingly divine, it is something to follow.
Evil's leadings can be prayerfully discerned as a sham or hollow.
Do not "shoot off" on a nudging faster than an object from a sling shot.
There will be hard lessons discovering holiness or what is not.
The Spirit of Truth illumines our eternal flame.
Blessed be the holy name.

The <u>Pillar and Foundation of Truth</u> is the church
and Jesus respectively we conclude by a scriptural search.
The church is the place we need to go for accountability.
Without it no Christian can have stability.
Sin demands to have a man alone.
Their seeds can then more easily be sown.
Sin loses its power in the context of light, truth, and accountability.

Our attendance at church is an important responsibility.
You usually have to respond to light
or sever yourself from it and get it out of sight.
There is much scripture and advice to heed.
We can get honest about our need
for God or die in the state of sin.
Thus, to eternal joy or unfathomable chagrin!
We can get honest that the Holy Spirit is guiding us must be an actuality
or die to a deadening state of spirituality.
Thus the pillar
is a vital filler.
Jesus is a base and foundation
of life and its vivification.

Spiritual Warfare: Confronting the Enemy – The Breastplate of Righteousness
July 30, 1991

Of the Christian's armor we need to tell.
The breastplate of righteousness protects us well.
When the enemy shoots straight for the heart,
Satan can't tear the breastplate or you apart.
A right standing with God defines righteousness.
This was accomplished through Jesus's perfectness.
Because of Christ your breastplate will last,
but there are two ways Satan can give it a blast.
Against your breastplate he can't do an elimination,
but with cunning and guile he'll work on distortion.
Evil will feed and distort your conjectures.
Let us look at two such distorted pictures.
Your spirituality can surely regress
if Satan can skew you on your thoughts of <u>righteousness</u>.

If of your own righteousness you are very <u>prideful</u>,
your need of a savior approaches null.
Isaiah 64:6 says our righteousness is filthy rags.
What is the worth of a whole bunch of these bags?
The blood of Christ can cleanse the filthiest heart.
Herein does sin and its ugly penalty depart.
But the enemy wants us to think we are always right.
Always blame others – we're right – their own plight.
This naturally causes disharmony.
An army is ineffective if it has no unity.
They make you think that if you fail, you lose.

You must never lose!
Our enemy wants us to think God owes us because we are good..
The Lord is not treating me as He should!
When we feel righteousness on our own,
we have very little need for the Lord on the throne.

The other trick is to make us feel <u>hopeless</u>.
Our position is one without any secureness!
Satan tries to convince us Jesus is not good enough.
We are just too bad, miserably wretched, and such stuff.
"God could never accept me.
From the consequences of sin, I could never be free!"
But the wonderful grace reaches out to the most defiled.
No matter how high your sins seem to be piled,
we must place the full righteousness
of Jesus on us and rely on His completeness.
If one is weighed down by the load of sin,
he will become ineffective while occupied with a great mental chagrin.
If we think of all of our sins of commission,
and also contemplate those of omission,
we can feel quite hopeless.
Thinking of nothing else could cause one to spiritually regress.
Satan also wants you to feel the temptation
is as bad as the sin – though it was only an evil fed rumination.
The enemy wants to keep you in a hopeless state.
Your spiritual climb will then more resemble fate.
But this is all an evil lie and sham.
We can claim victory and hope worshipping the great "I am."

Spiritual Warfare: Confronting the enemy – Sure Footing
September 8, 1991

Because of the gospel of peace, we can stand firm.
There are two points we need to affirm.
In the game of tug-of-war, a sure principle is found.
He who slips loses ground.
With the preparation of the gospel of peace our feet need to be shod.
You will then better over battleground more victoriously trod.
Some points about peace we shall consider two.
To enhance our footing, it should surely do.

By the awesome and wonder of God <u>we experience peace</u>.
Assurance of salvation in me can never cease.
It is by Christ our enemy did suffer defeat.
"God will crush Satan shortly under our feet."

We are justified through faith and have peace with God – our entry point.
Then we are to follow the path God does appoint.
We can rest on the assurance
we have peace with God for our entire worldly endurance.
The experience of peace helps us go through life
and is our wonderful secret in enduring tribulation and strife.
We need to lift our guard each day.
We experience peace when we pray.
We experience peace when in a relationship
with God and not by our deeds or words across the lip.

Our experience of peace gives us sure footing. (1)
It needs to grow like the oak for a deep rooting.
This strengthens our permanence.
Our trust in Christ needs to be a deep-rooted oak in its stance.
A good lesson from the Sumo wrestler can be found.
The object is to stand your ground.
He tries to knock his opponent out of the ring.
With the shield of faith we give Satan's darts a repelling fling.
Without a shield the darts can throw you back.
You will be thrown from the ring and off your spiritual track.

Our experience of peace also gives us mobility. (2)
This is in regard to a circumstantial adaptability.
To keep us from temptation
running is sometimes the only proper motion.
When losing ground on sin's slope,
applying the track shoes to flee is your only hope.
Know that we need to flee temptation,
but not spiritual battles – a truthful realization.
God has called us to
battles for our Christian growth the gospel writers knew.
Our assurance is that God is in control and on the throne.
Pity many Christians try to go it alone.
Confronting the enemy requires sure footing.
Your inner peace needs to be like the oak tree's deep rooting.

Spiritual Warfare: Confronting the Enemy –
The Shield of Faith
September 14, 1991

God provides complete protection
from the worst the enemy can throw at us in intended subjection.
Surely one must realize the situation does demand

us to use all resources at hand.
Our understanding should advance you should agree
if we consider points of three.

Flaming arrow: high tech weaponry of the enemy.
Satan having high-tech weaponry should be no surprising discovery.
Man invents things for good.
To use them for evil you should think Satan surely would.
Consider dynamite, the atom smasher, or t-v.
They can readily be misused you should agree.
Satan wants to devour us or take us out of the battle.
He is not here simply to give your "cage a rattle."
Church members fighting one another is no small whim.
He instigates this since they can't directly fight him.
When worship becomes a drudgery,
we are down and out of the battle to quite a degree.
Satan wants to rob us of our job, that adversarial destroyer.
That is, our job as Christ's warrior.
Satan is constantly trying to cause a moral lapse in the ministers
or any of the church leaders.
Then onlookers may say, "If that is supposed to be the ideal church,
I will continue my search."
He wins when he merely keeps us too busy to develop our Christian growth.
So the seeds of ideas for many activities he soweth.
Another arrow is sniping at us and wounding one
and causing others to attend him and thus a diversion has well begun.
Then in taking some out of the battle he has success.
He wishes to make the active Christian warriors ever less.
Here and there a few well aimed flaming arrows.
Always to get fewer to walk the straights and narrows.

The Shield of Faith: Complete Protection from God.
Fully adequate for us creatures who plod the sod.
Faith is abandoning our own self-reliance
and trusting someone else with full assurance.
The object of faith
needs to be worthy of our faith.
A poor penetrable shield would not be
worthy of our faith any warrior would readily agree.
God is all-powerful and can provide the necessary shield.
With that thought in mind we can all readily yield.
Taking up the shield we must do.
God is committed to protecting you.
Faith does not make us healthy, wealthy,
or without need in the lap of luxury.
We will have hardships, but nothing will separate
us from the love of God which He did create.

Our tendency is to rely on ourselves when we get out in front.
"I did well in enduring the battle's brunt."
Basic things keep us in balance – a must.
Worship, study, scriptural meditation, and trust!
Pondering how great God is keeps me in awe.
Satan can't pluck any from God's hand is the absolute law.
Usually faith is tested more in times of prosperity.
Too many (99% one said) turn a proud heart or to some improbity.
Hold hard and strong the shield of faith in confronting the enemy.
That shall produce spiritual prosperity.

Spiritual Warfare: Confronting the Enemy – The Helmut of Salvation

September 21, 1991

Our salvation in Christ gives us protection for our mind.
An application to several aspects a meditation will profitably find.
Our thinking can't here reach perfection,
but unto a few negative things we need not be in subjection.
Your mind and logic Satan will constantly try to dishevel.
By a study of the Word your mind can rise to a higher level.
Let us consider "protection against" by three points.
Through study and meditation, a peace the Savior appoints.

We have a protection <u>against</u> <u>doubt</u>.
Doubt is the enemy's favorite mental route.
By the Holy Spirit we are sealed.
No power is greater so salvation can't be unsealed.
By keeping you out of the Word, Satan can make you play the dunce.
The atonement of Jesus was perfect and He only had to die once.
Hebrews 6 states that if we could fall away, we could not be renewed.
Chapter 6 by any doubter needs to be reviewed.
A born again believer the Holy Spirit does indwell.
The Holy Spirit can no one ever expel.
The Holy Spirit can no one "sin out" or "kick out."
The assurance of salvation should have absolutely no doubt.
If the false rumor is by any of you heard,
tell the speaker to shush and get into the Word!

We have protection <u>against</u> <u>doublemindedness</u>.
Some thinking could retard your spiritual growth or cause you to regress.
James wrote "A double minded man is unstable in all of his ways."
Such shall not have many spiritually profitable days.
To trust in the Lord and His Word you must give it your all

or Satan will be on hand to aid and abet you in a fall.
You are double minded if your belief is only 90%.
God is able who is omnipotent, omniscient, and omnipresent.
What God promises shall be done – 100% sure.
There is no room for doubt or chance – you must concur.

We lastly have protection <u>against</u> <u>despair</u>.
This feeling comes naturally and our emotions need repair.
Problems mount and we feel we have lost all hope or confidence.
Solutions by human efforts have no expectance.
The state of the world is very wretched and sour.
So useless is the attempted correction by human power.
Wickedness is so rampant and at large.
Rejoice – the Lord is in charge.
Satan's force is one that we alone can't cope
with, but an omnipotent God stays our hope.
Evil will run its course until the Lord's time is full.
Hallelujah, amen, the Lord has complete control.

Spiritual Warfare: Confronting the Enemy – The Sword of the Spirit

September 22, 1991

Over souls and against time we are in a race.
With our armor in place
we more than defend.
Preparation has a useful end.
We take the battle to the enemy!
A soldier's end is not just to be always ready.
Never let the enemy dictate
the terms of battle as this may lead to fate.
We need to take up the offensive.
Indeed, the study of spiritual warfare is quite comprehensive.
The Word of God is the sword with which we can be armed.
Without it you will be like the snake the piper charmed.
Let us consider two things we need to be.
We can be more prepared for battle you should agree.

Be equipped is point one.
Without being armed, dressed, set, primed, and attuned a battle can't be begun.
The pieces of armor can't be odd and incompatible.
Jesus used knowledge in the wilderness against temptation.
What we have – the Word - ready for application.
All of the other pieces need to be in place

before the sword can be used with a battle before one's face.
The seven sons of Sceva did not have on the helmet of salvation
so their outcome was a predictable conclusion.
If you rely on your own righteousness
you will end up prideful, inadequate, and your battle will surely regress.
For failure we do not wish to labor or toil in vain.
So with the right mind we can battle that Christ might gain.

Be skilled is point two.
No substitute for training will do.
We have to plan to use our training to stimulate our motivation.
Use a skill and knowledge and put it to a state of activation.
We also want to know how to wield our sword.
There can be awesome results from applying the Word.
We need to turn to the Word for specific answers to specific situations.
Otherwise we use principles to make applications.
It is like deciding right or wrong from a code of ethics.
Knowledge can become like a routine working of systematics.
It has to be made a regular part
of our lives that knowledge can fully impart.
We have to build on God's Word as a life preparation.
The Christian experience is one of a never-ending education.
Our Christian life will be a better trip.
Our handle on the Word becomes a tight grip.
It would readily seem a truth – not a jive
if someone says a grip requires all fingers, a full five.
Hear, read, study, memorize, and meditate.
For getting a good grip there is no alternate.
The enemy wants to prevent you from being filled.
They dread the warrior you can be if you become very skilled.

Spiritual Warfare: Confronting the Enemy –
The Greatest Weapon of All
September 28, 1991

A good soldier likes to be well-protected and armed.
He will have a smaller chance of being harmed.
But armor is only for the defensive,
he must also go on the offensive.
It would be quite an infidel
who would think he did not need good weapons in his arsenal.
For the greatest weapon we need take great interest and care.
It is the power of prayer!
If we were really convinced, how would we pray?

Though there are more, let us consider four points this day.

Certainly <u>with</u> <u>all</u> <u>kinds</u> <u>of</u> <u>prayers</u> <u>and</u> <u>requests</u>.
Petitioning God is the key to spiritual conquests.
Now some might have a fit
that this does not mean the selfish wants of "name it and claim it."
William Cowper wrote, "Restraining prayer, we cease to fight,
prayer keeps the Christian's armor bright,
and Satan trembles when he sees
the weakest saint on his knees."
If a good prayer warrior could envision 1000 spiritual tasks,
then 1000 things he asks.

We would pray <u>on</u> <u>all</u> <u>occasions,</u>
But not with the idea of making selfish supplications.
Perhaps those who pray a lot could tell
that things seem to go generally well.
But much prayer is not to gain the life of charm
where one sees neither testing or harm.
More simply a prayer warrior as such
gets to see the Lord working in much.
To God does prayer draw one nearer
and our relationship to Him will become dearer.
There are so many bad situations and people in need.
Lending a prayer is surely a good deed.
It is written, "Ye have not
because ye ask not."
No occasion is too small because God does care
about even numbering your hair.

We would also pray <u>with</u> <u>all</u> <u>perseverance</u>.
There would be great reward for prayerful endurance.
Those who pray the most will find
God answers what is allowable in His mind.
Where great numbers of saints are gathered on their knees
will be the place of greatest results that one sees.
God loves to see tenacity or singleness of purpose with constancy.
With all resoluteness we need to request what could be to God's glory.
Indeed, those who pray with great resolve and vigor
can of an assurance of value proceed with ever more rigor.

And finally, we need to pray <u>for</u> <u>all</u> <u>the</u> <u>saints</u>.
As one without nourishment easily faints.
We need to request that each one can stand.
Much help the situation does surely demand.
For the more we lift up, one by one,
they will end up with more battles won.

All the saints comprise the family.
For all we need to pray for spiritual growth and safety.
We need to pray every day
that the devouring lion be held at bay.
For our many needs to the Father and the Lord Jesus we need to call.
Prayer is the greatest weapon of all.

Getting You Twice
October 8, 1991

Surely with sin you will be enticed.
With extraordinary attractiveness it will be spiced.
The evil angels are at hand.
They have inundated our land.
Some may think this absurd,
but Isaiah wrote the dragon brought forth one third.
They are the cause of our strife.
With a tempting angel you are "married to" for life.
Your mind with evil, lust, or temptation they do feed.
We know that in much they succeed.
They keep nursing bad thoughts along.
The object is to make you go wrong.

It eventually comes down to a choice.
You reject the thought or do the deed and they rejoice.
They will accentuate the feelings of lust and desire.
They can really flame a passionate fire.
You have heard, "Bad people have more fun."
This is no mere, harmless pun.
Sin for a season has its cost.
God's blessings or rewards will be lost.
They have the power to blind you to what is consequential.
They want to feed you with like things that could be sequential.

Now if you rebuke the thought
they become very distraught.
In fact, it would be better to deal with the mad hatter.
Your acceptance or rejection does greatly matter.
"You should not be thinking of that, vile wretch," they inject.
Now guilt comes to mind as you reflect.
Of such feelings and thoughts, they will be the source
if you chose not their desired course.
Expel the thought and don't feel guilty is my advice.
If you feel guilty or rotten, they are getting you twice.
Getting you to just think about sin will not suffice.

The "guilt trip" is getting you twice.

A Greater Than Mandrake
November 29, 1991

A certain character was more than an amusement.
He was his own fighting regiment.
He was a hypnotist and you could see
his power was of no small degree.
His character was a crime-fighter.
He was a virtuous, stalwart up-righter.
His opponents were succumbed by fear
or an imagined earth swallowing or net that did not actually appear.
This was the greatest exhibit of the power of suggestion.
His mental defenses were as good as a bastion.
In that all under his power fell,
restoration of justice went very well.

Now there is a greater hypnotist that can appall
and mighty Mandrake seemingly has no power at all.
The spiritual battle today
is a mind war in which many forces play.
Satan and his angels are what you should find
to be the force trying to control your mind.
They can surely exert actual power.
Their force is one we need to studiously scour.
But know that their power of suggestion
goes far beyond your mere expectation.
Through sensuous desires and lusts, they wish to control
your actions and destiny of your soul.
They are the masters of illusion
and are very good at beguiling you with delusion.
Though in church your alertness you would keep,
who do you suppose is making you fall asleep?
They can turn a fault or a grudge into an unbearable load
that only the Lord can unload.
Some of these spiritual things seem only to be an illusion,
but there is some kind of actuality well beyond delusion.
Their force shall never abate.
They are here to wreak havoc, destruction, and fate.
Between Christians they would change enmity into a mountain.
In creating divisiveness, they are an endless fountain.
Do not be surprised that some trivialness
is no longer a nothingness.
These delusions can lead to one's plight.

We must look to God for healing and insight.
By being passive you let evil take command.
Those who prayerfully seek God shall have the upper hand.
You will not disarm them or make them go away.
They will always be present and meddling every day.
In actual effect Mandrake's power was an effective fake.
Take heed – Satan is a greater than Mandrake.

On a Blood Trail
January 27, 1992

Consider a hungry lion on a blood trail.
It does not quit or think it would fail.
The sight of blood has more than appeal.
It becomes a labor of utmost ardor and zeal.
With singleness of mind it goes forth to pursue.
To exert all wile, cunning, and fervor too.
No worry of how much time it will spend.
It only considers the desired end.
So once on a blood trail, it would be a rare day
that the lion does not catch its prey.
Take a moment to reflect and pause.
Could any animal be more dedicated to a cause?

Now consider the Christian and his mission.
To build the church and exact edification.
How dedicated is your pursuit?
Is laziness a charge you could easily refute?
The lion is the doer and the catcher,
but you were only intended to be a fisher.
You only go forth with rod and line,
whatever be the Lord's end shall be fine.
Does a distraction easily draw you off course?
Are you importantly drawing upon every resource?
The lion does not carelessly stalk.
Neither should careless describe your walk.

Lost souls are the fisher's prey.
Expanding the body makes for a joyous day.
Certainly you learned along the way
that the Christian is another hunter's prey.
Far greater than the lion's is his resolve.
The church is an object to dissolve.
He wishes he were the great potentate.
The church would be a thing to victoriously annihilate.

The church shall never fail.
The God of all is the power that does prevail.
Upon evil one can't merely frown.
They can far greater than slow you down.
Negligence can have a great cost.
Some Christian testimonies are being destroyed and lost.
Again I say – take time to reflect and pause.
Great powers are each pursuing their cause.
Put on all the armor of the Christian warrior.
You have been chosen to be a good news bearer.
The hunt shall be lost by the weak-willed and frail.
Remember that the roaring lion is hot on your blood trail.

The Seven Son of Sceva
November 24, 1990

Many miracles by Paul were wrought.
The sick were healed as well as taught.
At simple commands Paul was very deft.
Evil spirits in people then immediately left.
To proclaim God and show divine power was Paul's commission.
Diseases and evil spirits were both in submission.

The seven sons of Sceva were vagabonds indeed.
For exorcism many had a need.
Each wanted to hew himself a nice piece of the stone reputation.
They thought it could easily be done by imitation.
"Come out evil spirit by Jesus who Paul preaches," we adjure.
The spirit came forth in an undesirable cure.
It leaped upon them, overcame them, and prevailed.
In something here, they sure failed.
They fled out of the house naked and lamed.
In their deed they did not become famed.

For wisdom and instruction, they needed an infusion.
They sought to imitate to their own confusion.
This was a power to which they were strangers.
They found out these evil spirits were powerful "derangers."
Be not like the seven sons and remain ignorant fools.
Much spiritual knowledge needs to be our possession.
There is a fate far worse than folly in every worldly obsession.

Othniel, Gideon, and Samson
December 3, 1990

Oh Christian, you are very gifted today.
From scripture this I can say.
Though not as empowered as the heavenly host,
by scripture's men of old you are gifted more than most.
The church to them was a hinted mystery.
Now you look back on many years of church history.
You need to do a humble search.

You have a divine gift to help edify the church.
To the body it will be a great cost
if you act like you are gift less or yours is lost.
But the greatest gift by most anyone's telling
is that you have the Holy Spirit which is indwelling.
Yea, you should be thankful and greatly care
that you have a gift which was once very rare.
As history was read or seen
it can be noted that Israel had judges numbering thirteen.
By scripture we do see
that Othniel, Gideon, and Samson were a special three.
For sin Israel was delivered into the enemy's hand
until there was repentance across the land.
When the children cried unto the Lord,
He raised up Othniel, the first judge, as a reward.
"The Spirit of the Lord came upon him," we read.
The land had rest 40 years and oppression did cede.

The Spirit of the Lord came upon Gideon.
The Lord raised him up to face the children of Midian.
For paganism Israel was again "in a fix."
God delivered them by Gideon, judge number six.
For a special judge and person, you make two.
They make a trio, so one more is due.

For Samson in Judges ch. 13, it was good and bad.
Though specially gifted, much of his life was sad.
He was great but also a wayward warrior.
Of his enemy he was the great destroyer.
The Spirit came upon him and he had great power.
He wreaked a lot of havoc in a single hour.
To write of Samson, I may return.
There is much from him to learn.
Samson was the privileged third, judge 13, and the last.
After him the Holy Spirit, a judge became a thing of the past.

Samson: The Wayward Warrior
December 4-7, 1990

Samson was chosen to be a Nazarite from the womb.
He was to be such all of the way to the tomb.
Even his mother was not to have wine or strong drink.
Of a Nazarite's life she was to be aware of and constantly think.
An angel said she would conceive and bear a son.
She was yet barren and thought she would ever have none.

The angel spoke and appeared twice.
It went up in the fire of an offering and came not thrice.

Samson's greatest enemy appeared to be lust.
He was indeed overcome by it and went spiritually bust.
He wanted his parents to haste and get him a pagan for a wife "now."
In this Samson did desecrate his Nazarite vow.
Now any Bible reader should frown.
From this point his spiritual life did spiral down.
For forty years the freedom of the people did pause.
To deliver Israel from the Philistines was a special cause.
He had a special childhood.
His parents raised him as they should.
Samson was given special courage we could say.
He killed 2000 with the jawbone of an ass in one day.

From scripture we can tell
there are at least eight reasons why he fell.
He disregarded his parents who were quite wise.
Taking a pagan wife was something all should despise.
He never learned how to submit to and obey the God-ordained life.
This led to tragedy way beyond mere strife.
He desecrated his vows in more than one way.
Besides a pagan wife he touched a dead lion one day.
He destroyed his testimony by his uncontrolled rage.
A blinded sense of righteousness would not be in any sage.
Solving Samson's riddle caused 30 changes of raiment as a gain.
The infuriated Samson burned down much of their grain.
He dulled his spiritual senses we must lament.
His devotional and prayer life seemed to be non-existent.
It is easy to see in this story
that Samson desired his own glory.
Over killing a thousand he made up a song.
Giving himself all of the credit was wrong.
In his inability to subdue his lust he defiled his mind.
He took several desirous women of a wrong kind.
To telling Delilah the secret of his strength he did bow.
His uncut hair was the sole remaining element of his vow.
In disclosing his secrets, he was not wise.
This ultimately caused his demise.

Samson appeared to have had little spiritual root.
His life was one of meager fruit.
He had been a strong man for twenty years.
Now he was utterly weakened, humiliated, and reduced to tears.
Because the Spirit of God did depart,
there was probably no joy in his heart.

His hair was cut, he was chained up and lost his eyes.
Hardly a good ending one would surmise.
In Samson's capture the Philistines were revenged.
Perhaps Samson wanted God's honor to be avenged.
He prayed for strength to push the two columns with all of his might.
More than 3000 idolaters fell and met their plight.
Perhaps Samson's final spiritual state was redressed.
It was little fruit to come from a life so uniquely blessed.

His life story is not all tragic you should find.
His greatest contribution lies in the warnings his life leaves behind.
If you are sin's target,
flee from it before your life turns to regret.
His study can be a very helpful session.
From it we can draw many a lesson.

God uses us in spite of our sin.
In sinfulness we will end as well begin.
Blessing does not come because of our "great purity."
Behind old rags our righteousness lies in obscurity.
The Lord's work through Samson was not for faithfulness
or any spiritual steadfastness.
It would be a similar story
that it was for God's glory.
Samson imposed upon God's grace.
God is not around for an "all for me" race.

God is not patient forever with sinful living.
He is not just loving and infinitely forgiving.
God will eventually remove us from action.
He may much sooner disable us from getting sinful satisfaction.
If the only person we can serve is self,
God will have to put us on the shelf.

We reap what we sow.
God is not mocked you should know.
The bounteous crop of the seeds of sin is defeat,
though for a while we seem to have a delightful treat.
We have a choice as to what we can engender.
To think you are "getting by" makes you a foolish pretender.
God looks for obedience.
May God's will and purpose be our allegiance.
Forgiveness results from repentance,
but not without consequence.
Any Bible scholar should say
that for prolonged disobedience there is a price to pay.
Because you are not struck by a great physical infirmity,

evil may give you a false feeling of indemnity.
That all make mistakes is a sure declaratory.
A mistake does not write the living spiritual obituary.

Even in our times of weakness and failure,
we can still be the channel of God's power, to be sure.
It was something Samson could do
and it can be true for you.
For when we are weak, God is still strong.
It is only important that we to Him do belong.

Now most would surely believe
that it is with our full potential we should achieve.
Samson is a good example you should concur
that a minimal blessing could only occur.
If it is God's full blessing you want to see Him giving,
it will only come with disciplined living.
The story of Samson has many lessons to tell.
Heed them and you will do quite well.

Mene, Mene, Tekel?
December 9, 1990

Mene, mene, tekel, one more word will do.
What would it be if it were just for you?
For king Belshazzar it was originally written.
He lacked so he had to be smitten.
Only fingers of a man's hand wrote on the wall.
He defiled the temple vessels and shortly thereafter took a fall.
For judgment God will not forever wait.
Many need to change their ways before it is too late.

You should be conjecturing
whether in balance you would be found wanting.
Somehow, some way God will make a correction.
To the power of the same hand you are in subjection.
Being a real woman or man
is not going for all of the gusto you can.
If from all the things of God you flee,
you may not have much time to bow the knee.
If you are going down a sinful, wicked path,
you will be under a holy God's wrath.
Mene, God has numbered your days to cut it short.
Tekel, you are found wanting is the report.
If these two words are not for you, it is great.

But if they are, consider your pending fate.

A Holy Ghost Revival???
December 25, 1990

I saw a church advertise "A Holy Ghost Revival."
Is the Holy Ghost near dead or require resuscitation for survival?
You are indeed asylum level crazy
if you think spirituality lacks because the Holy Ghost is lazy.
Your errancy is long
and you have things all wrong.
Scripture must be well-read and often heard
to know truth and sway one from dogma that is absurd.
If one be carnal it is because his heart
and God are yet far, far apart.
The Word must for years and years be studied and learned
for spiritual truths to be correctly discerned.
Evil really has you on a wild loop
if you think spirituality comes as fast as instant soup.
Sanctification is a long gradual process where we study and pray.
Maturity comes not like fast burgers on a silver tray.
Unless your prayer be on your knees every day,
you have not even learned how the humble pray.

Pray to the Father in the name of the Son.
It is God the Holy Spirit's power by which souls are won.
Never does the Word say
"Pray unto the Holy Spirit this day."
If you ask amiss, you are the clay demanding of the Potter.
Evil has gobbled your common sense like cattle do their fodder.

Scaling mountains to gain spiritual height
comes not by simple human might.
Ascending to the "high country" is a long, arduous trip.
You will often stumble and slip.
Many will go askew
and never attain a "high country" view.
Many will learn too late
they called not upon God to prevent evil from causing their fate.
If you are one calling for "A Holy Ghost revival,"
I indeed fear for your spiritual survival.

Time – The Panzer Tank
January 4, 1991

The sure marching Panzer tank
going on without a request or one thank.
Consider that you and time will make a sure mark.
Deliberate the journey upon which you will embark.
The tank goes on even if you are still.
Think of the tossed stone rippling upon the rill.
It seems to die in a dissipating force.
But for eternity, time has a Panzer marking course.
You go forth to conquer and make a quest.
Will your route be one to rue or one that will be blessed?
It will be a pity if your run be one you will grieve
or worse yet you leave another Ambleve.
All deeds ripple into eternity.
God remembers all - of guaranteed surety.
The course can be a glorious crusade
or one that heaven should dissuade.
Unless Jesus gives you direction,
you will course onto an indeterminable destruction.
Your course will be more properly themed
if by the blood of the Lamb you have been redeemed.
At the end you will get out to eternal night
or heaven's everlasting light.
Your course will be one to deplore
unless you finally get to heaven's shore.
Will you have much left to admire
when all of your deeds pass through the judgmental fire?
To give account of all days it will be demanded.
Consider going into eternity and being empty-handed.
Meditate well the strategy before your way.
Soon the Panzer tank will conquer another day.

Of or from the Church
January 6, 1991

For ministering to people there is so much to do.
Surely there is something for you.
Servanthood is to be blended with the spiritual.
The "state" does things in a matter somewhat of a ritual.
In caring for the needy the church has somewhat failed.
For success the "state" oft falters or gets derailed.
Over success evil may easily trod

if things are done apart from God.
To decide is usually an easy task.
Is the ministering arm of or from the church I ask?
Make not the physical provision good but the spiritual a gyp.
All need be brought into the church fellowship.
If with the fellow spiritual workers, you can't discuss doctrine,
I deem you made an incorrect intertwine.
With fellow workers we need to be in accord.
No great spiritual ministry will be wrought in discord.
Jesus and his disciples comprised a working team.
From this we best work as a church body I deem.
Jesus' spiritual ministry was first.
He later responded to hunger and thirst.
Often people in a studying church group are closely knit.
Can they work as a pregnancy crisis unit?
Many tithe as a good deed.
Do they go to the hurting and those with a real need?
To get involved you will have to be bold.
Great blessings come about then, it is commonly told.
Strive to be the church's outreaching, outworking arm.
Look to God for provision and fear not harm.

On the Golden Years
February 8, 1991

Doubtless many have their greatest fears
in looking forward to their golden years.
Looking ahead
is not something the saint should dread.
Alexander Pope wrote of the pain and the bliss.
He wrote not in a manner of "hit or miss."
It will be a glorious hour
when we see Jesus in His full power.
The spirit created by God as a "flame"
will be quite splendid without the mortal frame.
Death for the Christian is God's intended goal.
Learn now well that your spiritual growth is made whole.
Evil would have you think death is something to deplore.
Nay, Christian, indescribable delight to reach heaven's shore.

Yea, eventually the physical body shall fail.
Let God's spiritual engendering prevail.
This mortal body death shall demand.
But how glorious will be the moment we come up to Beulah land.
For some the view of death is quite morose.

But Christian, to God you can now become very close.
To God we need to all draw nearer.
Looking to see the trinity should become dearer.
Our radiance like the blooming flower does all too soon pass.
For what awaits, the world's best can't surpass.
Let it stay your mind
that the body will only shortly lag behind
even though no trace of you will be found
as it becomes covered by the ground.
But, look further ahead and God be praised!
Indescribable will be the glorious body reunited and raised.
Death is a scene the ignorant gruesomely paints.
Nothing is more precious to God than the death of his saints.
Look now to God to vanquish your needless fears
as you graciously approach the golden years.

The Weeping Wall
February 10, 1991

It was from a national park I think.
To such the picture would seem to link.
It was titled "The Weeping Wall."
Many springs leaked out of the mountainside so tall.
Think if it also had a voice.
Would your passing by cause it to cry or rejoice?
The power of sin too many victims does keep.
For you the wall needs to weep.
What think you of the majority that pass by?
Indeed, the wall should surely cry.
Ponder life, oh sinful man.
You may one day go to the mountainous west.
If it be spring, the wall shall weep at its best.
Is your life one you should appall?
Well then should cry the weeping wall.
Better you say, "I am a saved, sanctified, Christly brother.
Oh, weeping wall, save your tears for another."

Before His Face
February 18, 1991

To some things we can ponder
and get not beyond unbelievable wonder.

Think of creating a universe.
One, man could never completely traverse.
All parts to God are known and in complete control.
The Regulator and Observer is one such role.

No sparrow does unknowingly drop
or a speck of slush without notice does plop.
Consider He is the artificer of all snowflakes.
Power beyond comprehension it takes.
His face is about every high mountain
and observes every snowmaker and fountain.
No snowflake occurs by chance.
No proof can be given to this foolish idea some do advance.
Every square inch of the world must be seen
or parts would have no snowflakes it would otherwise mean.

The snowflakes, I say, illustrate His presence.
Try to show me a place of His absence.
His Glory is bigger than the Milky Way.
Isaiah saw Him in a vision on the throne one day.
To be seen He is relatively small
or no human could see His "all."
Man shall one day look upon God's face.
So, heed well how you run life's race.
You will know God is "all present" and "all knowing."
It is to us mostly now a reading.
We can't see what God does see
or know what He knows to any substantial degree.

All angels – whitely attired and the fallen – do his bidding.
There can be none that are not obeying.
God sees the rippling in every rill
and causes storms and then makes them still.
On this we would write infinitely beyond our years.
Conclude nothing escapes Him – it surely appears.

Many now do scoff
and think God is so far off.
You foolish demented.
In your unbelief you are regimented.
You will later only see judgement instead of His grace.
You will learn too late all was before His face.

Out of the Nebula – The Christ
March 14, 1991

Darkness and fog abounded one night.
The boat tossed as in a pending probable plight.
The disciples were in the boat alone.
They had probable cause to moan.
Of no avail were their efforts to row.
In the distance a dark shadow.
"It is a ghost," they cried out of fear.
They could see Jesus as He came near.
When he stepped into the boat the wind did tame.
Out of the nebula the Christ came.

Consider a small idea in your head.
Coming perhaps by day or in your bed.
Just a tiny thought.
Measurable and as visible as naught.
It may be the urge to do a good deed.
Perhaps for even greater it is a divine seed.
For inception all things have their hour.
Nurture the thought to come forth in full power.
At first it may only bring
forth a rather small thing.

But in other things you could find
that God had something much greater in mind.
By human efforts the thought may very well fail.
Unknown greatness results if the Lord gives it sail.
A thought or little deed.
What results from a little mustard seed?
God is the accomplisher and the leaven
that can make your deed or renown reach to heaven.
I should be a writer I once said.
It came many years ago to my head.
Just a couple of seconds the thought took.
Now He shall bring it forth in a book.
For origin your thought or idea may be near the same.
Just haziness, but out of the nebula the Christ came!
Yea, a thought, a shadow, God's early plan – just an obscurity.
Then the work in bloom or Christ before us – how wondrous at maturity.

No One Understands
March 16, 1991

God has everyone go a different course.
He is definitely our courser, cause's source.
Upon other saints we can look.
Each life wends its way as a unique brook.
Some things only God and I know.
These things between us do not show.
For some things onlookers can never understand why.
To figure out a life is to figure out God – don't try!
Many saints have things they will not share.
We do not spill all to show people we care.

You need think, it is between God and me.
All is not for the world to see.
For some God has quite a different plan.
An unexplainable life may be such a woman or man.
We know not some people's comings and goings.
As impossible to see spiritual blessings and sowings.
We can't explain each traversing saint.
A full picture of discernment only God can paint.
Even one in the spirit (gone from the body) we could know.
Along in an invisible energy they each go.
We appear to see the "whole."
But friend, only God can see the soul!
Perhaps a frustrating segment of life lends much trauma.
We are totally at loss to understand each dilemma.
I perceive not the spiritual valleys and mountains.
So unique are all the saints' spiritual fountains.
I reflect and decide at last.
Much perception of my neighbor shall fleet on past.
The mind of God full perception demands.
Of all others "no one understands."

Where Were the Nine?
August 9, 1991

Not just a few in today's multitude
express not proper gratitude.
Somethings too many do not do
is say even a simple thank you.
Oh saint, do you reflect always on your misery?
You can daily thank God for an eternal destiny.

It is no small thing to be pulled from the path
of eternal wrath.
Far too many in their state of abundance do deplore
the fact that they have not even more.
Need you be a racer that no one can beat?
Think of the one with no feet.
Gratitude can be a great source of pleasantry.
Teaching children thankfulness is a necessity.
Perhaps you should count your blessings one by one.
You may be surprised at a long list when you are done.

Jesus went to a certain village one day.
Ten men who were lepers stood afar off the way.
"Have mercy on us, Master."
They knew He was no mere teacher.
Unto the priests they were sent.
They were cleansed as they went.
Down the road they quickly all trod.
Only one turned back and glorified God.
But He truly cleansed all ten.
Ah, perhaps it is still now as then.
Only one was grateful outwardly that all was fine.
But where were the nine?

Always on Target
October 22, 1991

Consider the ways of man.
Much happens in a matter of catch-as-catch-can.
People have goals, targets, and projected ends.
Along the way occur many revisions and amends.
Much seems to happen by luck, chance, or a lucky choice.
True that many people have talents, skills, or an articulate voice.
It sees to be an obvious fact to discover
that the more talented one will rise above another.
The more aggressive person or cheat
is hard to beat.
Though a few seem to have unlimited financial power,
They have no choice on death's hour.
To take your own life too soon you surely can,
but there will be no endless living woman or man.
A few things seem to boil down to chance or a bet,
because man can never be always on target.

Though you seem to each opt your own course,

life is directed by an invisible source.
All the earth and universe is observed and under supervision.
All fall under God's direction and provision.
Oh, self-made man of high power,
it is God's choice in you rising to rule or your dethroning hour.
You will one day discover
that a lot more than you thought was controlled by another.
To lose their life most do surely rue or hate,
but know that is God the Father that selects your date.
More important than your earthly kingdom or glory
is how you will spend eternity.
God makes a choice and has eternal power
that there is absolutely no wavering by a second in the appointed hour.
With God there is no guess or required debate.
He will execute your kingdom glory or fate.
Nothing boils down to a chance or bet
Because God is 100% always on target.

On Safari

November 3, 1991

Adventure some demand.
Indeed, obtained traversing the Lord's glorious land.
Only a few have adequate resources and money
to make more than one extended journey.
Though an annual travel be dear,
what about the rest of the year?

Now I would be remiss
if I said spiritual things are a constant bliss.
It doesn't take a genius to decide
that life is not just an adventurous train ride.
But amid the problems and toil,
I serve the King most royal.
Life is still life
and we must endure much strife.
But life is not just a laboring unto one's fate;
the Lord is our master and as well our help-mate.
For Him we live.
Purpose of life He does give.
Religion often leads to indifference.
Christianity from the heart makes all of the difference.
The Lord shall lead me in a lifetime adventure.
I'll not say I top all worldly feelings of drugs and pleasure.
Though many be led to sin by temptation and guile,

I find the Lord makes life worthwhile.
My eternal destiny is resolved.
Without it all true peace or hope would be dissolved.
Over the years times and things get changed.
By the Lord things get positively rearranged.
Though many look to the thrill of a new toy,
there is much to say for the intrinsic value of inner joy.
The Lord has for the obedient a wonderful itinerary.
Well, there is just no way of telling what is coming up on safari.

Etchings
November 22, 1991

Sit back to ponder and reflect.
View your paths in a manner circumspect.
Consider the lives you touch.
Some things matter little but others matter much.
You mark other people like an etching on a plate.
The marks are caused by how you relate.
Your own life will be an example to copy.
Will the pictures be deleterious or one to edify?

Should not your life be a plate ending up like a masterpiece.
Does the thought give you unrest or lend you peace?
If you be a plate as a "self-made" man,
it will be hap-hazard artistry in a manner of catch-as-catch-can.
Does Christ shape your thoughts and visage?
Is the Master progressing or did the work stop at some stage?
In time it can be told
you are Christ's workmanship to wonderfully behold.
Youth engrains in what they see.
The works before them influence as so what they will be.
We can each be a wonderful fascination
if the design and artistry are the Lord's composition.
The fine lines take great care to complete the intricacy.
The spirit and character are in some ways an amazing complexity.
A gentle word or a good deed make some kind of etching.
Do you think you are an example others will be admiring and copying?
Even little remarks make their marks like etching on a plate.
Consider whether you be Christ's masterpiece or a tragic fate.

Unknown Pioneers
February 16, 1992

Perhaps there is a great work or building you adore.
It was made by no small chore.
The workmanship was great.
Workers unknown whether yet alive or of late.
Some can say, "I remember the builders."
Just some plain workers.
Most often not listed by name
or enshrined or put on a plaque with a special frame.
Some of your work may be an important plus.
Your talent and gift may not make you famous,
but it does not mean you are not valuable.
With God all things will be rewardable.
"For God is not unrighteous to forget your work and labor of love."
The omnipresent God is not one to miss something being too far above.
In that you have ministered to the saints and do minister,
you are being recorded in a perfect register.
For many of the world and a few Christians fame
is probably the end of their game.
Not enough hard work might be the blame
that they can't exalt their own name.
We are not rewarded for fame, but for faithfulness.
Fame will be the end to which some will undoubtedly progress.
To make it a priority your spirituality may regress.
Just "doing it for Jesus" will be what God wishes to bless.
Do not worry or stop to think if you are among some volunteers.
A lot of things are wrought by unknown pioneers.

They Raised the Roof
February 22, 1992

This story is more than a simple lesson to bring.
Perception takes one beyond just the "main thing."
One can profitably meditate upon a law or creed
and see that there is more than just a "deed."
Healing the man on the cot was a wonderful thing you would agree.
Upon meditating we can actually see miracles of three.
To call something a miracle I rightly can
if it goes beyond the ability of a man.

The place was a house and might have been like a reception.
The first miracle was Jesus's all-knowing perception.

The faith of the four men He perceived.
People like such were well received.
Christianity is having concern
for one another like the four men you should discern.
The four were earnest and persistent.
In such a manner our walk should be consistent.
Does Jesus see faith and trust in us?
Great works without faith is no plus.
Without faith God is not pleased you read.
Yea, it is something often said.

Jesus also perceived the man's need.
For our sins we must all plead
to be saved from the consequential wrath
of a sinner not averted from doom's path.
There was a relationship between the outer healing
and the inner healing.
The physical body was made whole.
There was also healing for the soul.

Jesus also perceived the thoughts of the Pharisees.
They thought, "Who is this who speaks blasphemies?
Who can forgive sins but God alone?"
They thought Jesus was out of place walking in a forbidden zone.
Though Jesus did the works of God, they would not believe
nor would they see He was the anointed one they should receive.

The second miracle was the pardon of sin.
For a better way of redemption Jesus's ministry did begin.
Mankind in doing all of the sacrifices was at a loss.
There was a better way for us through the cross.
"Thy sins be forgiven thee."
Who else but God could remit sins or make a blind person see?
With a lot of "good talk" they could make a shower,
but surely next to Jesus they had no power.
To see so many miracles the Pharisees had no comment.
Now you shall ever lament.

To His third miracle they needed to "take off their hat."
"Get up and take your mat!"
Jesus can heal by speaking.
So too by just thinking.
The paralytic glorified God as he departed.
Surely wisdom and belief should have been more widely imparted.
You foolish ones who fell back
into your vain mental track.
You would have been more than ahead

to look well at the one who commanded the lame take up his bed.
The purpose of divine power working
in man is that they could thereby be praising.

Thus, a simple lesson to receive.
The wise can see there is much to perceive.
The fool's rejection shall carry him to plight.
The wise one goes beyond wisdom to insight.
You Pharisees saw, rejected, and went askew.
The paralytic saw, felt, believed, and spiritually grew.
A miracle of one blossomed into a spectrum of three.
An interesting observation would you agree?

Running the Race
June 28, 1992

Consider if you are or would be a jogger or a runner.
Perhaps your progress seems a bummer.
You liken the whole situation to your run.
It may seem boring, useless, and not much fun.
To others we will naturally make a comparison.
We will make conclusions before everything is over and done.
Oft we will not be satisfied with our pace.
Others will seemingly always win the race.
You will quickly notice this in income or position.
Perhaps you will also feel you always get more opposition.
Some in the world appear to always be on easy street.
You walk to a different beat.
Perhaps you and not they know your eternal destination.
You are making an unequal comparison.
Worldly wealth will be all they have towards eternity.
Surely you would not trade positions to get eternal misery.
Perhaps another person seems to get every reward.
Better that you are going the way of the Lord.
Salvation is not a position to put you always ahead.
Down quite a different track you will be led.
Only for the world are some running the race.
Better you just progress and at God's pace.

A Miracle, No Denial, But no Admission
July 3, 1992

Peter preached through Jesus the resurrection from the dead.
You have surely read.
Many of the people believed,
but the priests, Sadducees, and the Sanhedrin were grieved.
Of Jesus did Peter preach and tell.
An impotent man he also made well.
God's work was manifest most people could see.
Christ's power was shown and to a great degree.
"By what power, or by what name have ye done this?"
Upon hearing and seeing they remained amiss.
"The stone which was set at naught is become the head of the corner.
Neither is there salvation in any other."
The Sadducees perceived Peter and John to be unlearned
and ignorant men and they marveled.
"Indeed, a notable miracle has been done by them," to wit
"We can't deny it."

Salvation could have come to them in that hour.
Ponder what kept them away – surely Satan's power.
Jesus confirmed this fact in His parables.
Not overpowering enough were even his notable miracles.
Though a miracle was more than evident,
they wanted to reward the disciples with punishment.
The majority of people glorified
God and Jesus was greatly magnified.
How could you yet be so deceived?
By five thousand men was salvation received.
The Sadducees could perhaps think only of their religious position.
Holding another higher than them would lead to their own dissipation.
Pity you saw, but would not give admission.
This could have led to your salvation.
Ye who believe, give thanks, but also be aware
of the fact you could have been also in an evil snare.
We are all nothing and have no power in this spiritual contest.
Purely in grace and predestination did your salvation rest.
By God's choice were you allowed to make confession by your lips.
The multitude is held by evil grips.
Perhaps more will be released if more people pray.
The gospel of salvation must we convey.
The Sanhedrin and Sadducees most likely died in their sins.
We need shudder as we are mindful we have been saved from our sins.
Think of the many who by evil are kept in the dark.
Salvation is no simple path on which we randomly embark.
Pity you Sadducees, because of your "no admission,"

you received "no remission."

A Decree
July 5, 1992

Command that all seek God!
It may not be with a mere essential nod.
Wickedness has overrun this land.
A purging is in great demand.
Declare publicly everyone who proclaims Christ's name.
Let all of the rest be slain.
To those who think this is absurd,
know that before these words were several times heard.

You who seek to serve yourselves in lusts wholly,
know that God ever shall be and is holy.
Fearing eternity and God should be your desire.
All shall one day inherit heaven or hell fire.
In Asa's time (900 B.C.) the people were very depraved.
He sought God that many could be saved.
More wickedness would bring about God's destructive storms.
Asa responded with further and sweeping reforms.
The all-powerful God he did greatly fear.
He chose to live, prosper, and hold obedience very dear.
To repent and turn from sin the people were very glad.
Today's situation is very, very sad.
To seek God will bring about the best.
The Lord gave the land rest.
(To slay the wicked was a good thing
else God's wrath upon the whole land they would bring.)
God shall not just forever stand back.
Repentance or judgment shall roar as a locomotive down the track.
Oh, that God would save us before it is too late.
A wicked government and land shall bring about a great fate.
I pray that a revival is just ahead
or there will come something we all will dread.

Blessed be the Meditation
February 23, 1992

"May God bless the reading of His word."
This I have oft heard.

The reading is good you should surely see.
But it is not just for reading only.
A preacher is blessed by his study time
and with time I put together many a rhyme.
One source of my writings
is taking notes from sermons and teachings.
The notes are the poem's beginning state.
The Lord does wonderfully add when I further meditate.
A preacher inserting a bulletin outline is the best.
It gives the poem an initial frame and potential zest.
I have a basic organization.
You also can use them for further thought and edification.
Initial thoughts by notes comprise lines of only some.
Paralleling causes the other lines to come.
Neat ideas and things I get.
They are indeed from God you can surely bet.
Unique metaphors and illustrations bloom.
This is true for all you may assume.
Discernment and insight come by the Holy Spirit.
They are not just scarcely doled out by special merit.
You will discover meditation to be a delight
as God illumines His Word and wisdom's light.
Wisdom is not reserved for only a blessed few.
In thinking taking not enough time you will go askew.
Poems and lines of wisdom were not an instant shower.
I spent also many a hour.
Study is a thing with increasing marginal utility and returns.
There is more than what meets the eye the meditator learns.
"Blessed be the reading," we can say without hesitation.
The much greater is "blessed by the meditation."

Upon Meditation
February 27, 1992

I exhort all to more meditation.
You foolishly lose upon needless hesitation.
Contemplation gains it reward.
Know that it is a thing loved by the Lord.
Some fools hold meditation to be philosophical nonsense,
but it shall surely have its recompense.
It will be of God where added insight is from.
"Happy is the man that findeth wisdom,
and the man that getteth understanding."
So saith Solomon in his books of writing.
"For the merchandise of it is better

than the merchandise of silver,
and the gain thereof than fine gold."
So the wise one has told.
Study and meditation is the way a pastor
does magnificently and wonderfully minister.
Speak of the things of the Lord in your comings and goings.
Speaking of them from morning until night
shall be to you and God a great delight.
Only the knowledge of God can make one complete.
"Thou shall lie down and thy sleep shall by sweet."

Certain discussions can be unprofitable deals.
Beware lest a fool gets you needlessly spinning your wheels.
Some high-minded philosophers debate points of futility
as their discussions have no real utility.
Incline your ear unto what the Lord is saying.
You will thereby have a blessed wayfaring.
Surely know that a quick glance or look
will not lead you to expound forth a book.
Meditate and facts of one and one can come up with three.
Jesus said, "Ye shall know that the truth and the truth shall make you free."
Know that it is the Lord each time that does insightfully add
and you immediately as well as later will be very glad.

Chasing Illusions and Solutions
March 13, 1992

So, on what is your life's focus?
Some do no better than just cajole and do some hocus pocus.
So be one a hobo on the road
or a frantic executive ready to explode,
you are both in a dither
unless life is simply just to go hither and thither.
But, then the yon becomes a too complacent here,
And then, of course, that requires a new there.
So, the hobo hits the road again
and the exec invents a new deal to spin.
Perhaps fuller purpose will be down the road farther
or on top of the wealth that needs to be piled a bit higher.
Each one hoping to go just a tad
more and then they should be glad.
Some days contemplating purpose makes one sad,
if lucky, but quite a few have actually gone mad!
Oh, if one could merely lose his cool
instead of despair and insanity getting control and rule.

Yea, one needs to take great care
to stay out of the clutches of that deadly pair.
So, all in all, indeed, too much becomes an unfruitful mishap.
Surely by now someone should have written a good roadmap.
To catch purpose, satisfaction sure seems to compel,
but its as illusive as that darn Scarlet Pimpernel!
(He was a master of disguise.
He seemed to constantly vanish right before the "Frenchies'" eyes.)
So, purpose for many seems to be ahead and right in sight.
Then as one gets close, it is like a mirage which becomes dissipated light.

Not too surprisingly fortune and fame
become life's game.
It surely is a natural desire of almost every woman and man
to get or accumulate all you can.
There is a long way from a basic need
and getting extra just because it satisfies greed.
So many "nice things" seem in demand.
Attainment for some takes total command.
For too many life is only fattening a purse.
Yea, life can be described as a living curse.
Something is missing most do decide.
Outside things seem to be in control of my mad ride.
Inflation causes many to really labor.
A bad government is printing too much money you should concur.
For most and especially low wage earners this is real robbery.
Our congressmen retiring with multi-millions will not be in misery.
Many become victims of life in the fast lane.
They need to be hardy to bear a lot of pain.
After going around and around
no good or true purpose can be found.
It is not satisfying enough to set goals and make resolutions.
Purpose is not found by chasing illusions and solutions.

Oh, fruitless chaser, you should not find it so odd
that we were created to worship God.
Salvation comes only through Jesus's name.
God can set your focus and give you an aim.
Only a short time we live most would lament.
After this the judgment!
Only with Jesus as Lord will you discover your manifest destiny
as well as know where you will spend eternity.
True purpose will never come on the world's merry-go-round.
Stop chasing windmills and illusions and purpose in Christ will be found.

The Tip of the Iceberg
March 22, 1992

Consider life of your neighbor,
Christian brother, or sister.
We see only some of their walk
and perhaps more or less of them by their talk.
We really know little by their outside.
One's disposition and mental complex is hidden on the inside.
Much is like the iceberg you see.
Seven eighths is under the sea.
Invisible is most of life's complexity.
Understanding by observation is often a fruitless perplexity.
Comprehension is not something one can simply choose.
Have you not heard you must first walk a mile in your neighbor's shoes?
Perception of others seems to sometimes digress
as the greatest element of a Christian's walk is God's mysteriousness.
Insight into some things shall be a useless try.
God is infinitely above man and will always be too high.
Centuries ago English writers warned against rash judgment.
People will too often jump to verbalization they will soon lament.
But surely there are things we must try to understand.
To show love or care compassion does demand.
Outwardly some people are only sighing,
But on the inside, they are screaming or crying.
Some things people will not share.
Their inner ticking will not be laid bare.
Such are the spiritual ways.
Many parts can surely put one in a daze.
Spiritual development really has some intricate workings
and mysterious doings.
Take heed before you hastily give some "bad lip."
You are most likely seeing only the iceberg's tip.

Mustering the Resolve
March 28, 1992

Most know that work is not just working.
For a manager or office person there needs to be planning.
I see especially as an accountant/computer systems analyst.
Objectives or accomplishments oft need to be put on a list.
Now and then I appear to be daydreaming or in a reverie.
Systems development is creativity and imagery.
Knowledge plus intuitive ability

fuel one's creativity.
Beyond this most should find
that you often need to just work the mind.
When there are dozens of tasks at hand,
prioritizing is surely in demand.
"So very much to do," is the common talk.
Paul describes the slower "Christian walk."
When I list all of my desires I get a "wow."
To do most I know not how.
Priorities must one realistically face
or one will be like a mad charioteer never ending the race.

Studying the Word or following Christ is a decision.
Too many tasks or too little time invokes a rescission.
I reckon it unto reading John Milton.
A man of God a couple of centuries ago already gone on.
You will see quickly "Paradise Lost" is not a romantic novel
or just a reader or tale of someone trying to revel.
If such reading would similarly rank,
you will read much and end up a mental blank.
A slowing down and "stepping up" decisions must one involve.
It will require effort in mustering the resolve.
Thinking for some is way too much
work and a black plague to be avoided as such.
Christianity does not require that you be a real "brain."
Most in an unsuccessful manner would remain.
God works with all on their created level.
Averting your Christian walk is the task of the devil.
Surely each person can only go so high.
It is not chiefly enablement but how much you try.

Does not an athlete plan exercise and pain
for a later beneficial gain?
Your spirituality does also likewise greatly matter.
You will play the fool by not trying to go up Jacob's ladder.
The spiritual walk leads to spiritual maturity.
You are positioning yourself for eternity!
No care of what is done for Christ or what will happen tomorrow
will absolutely bring about the later sorrow.
Going to college or tech for most is not an obsession.
It is an advancement to a better job or higher profession.
It takes time and effort to develop such skills.
Thus, one also advances by prayer, study, and memorization drills.
Things require money and most want to be higher paid.
They try to advance and in this not be delayed.
So, if planning is worthwhile for a job for 40 years,
will not carelessness for eternity cause many tears?

Christian growth is not just effort for an eternal obscurity,
but one can take joy in walking in the present spiritual "high country."
Your effort shall surely not just be some going askew.
The Lord rewards with an insightful spiritual view.
Along the way there will be times of great frustration.
Life is otherwise also as such so proceed without hesitation.
Some things will be mysteries you can't solve.
For the rest it is a matter of mustering the resolve.

A Good Life – Balanced and Harmonious
March 28, 1992

Some people are really messed up, to say the least.
They sow a lot of wild oats and take in fast rising yeast.
Life is mostly reveling and seeking wild satisfaction.
Many will surely end with some form of destruction.
Good that some find life should be a better deal.
They go about returning to an even keel.
They know they must go about an alteration.
It readily appears that most things must be done in moderation.
Returning to normal may be a great task.
No more drinking from the cup drawn from extremity's cask.
Getting straightened out becomes a great chore.
How wonderful to discover life is worth living once more!

Thus, all should ponder if everything is in balance.
This is not a matter of luck or chance.
There needs to be some deliberation,
weighing things in the balance, and some good self-examination.
Nothing dare to be too consuming.
Neither upon time or resources can it be too demanding.
One should feel that all things are in-tune and harmonious.
"Everything" may not be quite so obvious.
Fine-tuning is a topic to produce a long dissertation.
One must first look at reasonableness and defining moderation.
Also, a look-see to norms, social morés, and verities.
Avoid not meditating sin and iniquities.
We can easily be blinded to truth and morality.
Be not Quixotic and run from the mirror of reality.
For a truth and a norm nothing can better fit
than the Word of God and the Holy Spirit.
Facts and what "should be" can oft belie.
All can be deceived by a Satanic lie.
A third of heaven did he deceive.
The correct standard without God is impossible to conceive.

Only God can really bring about balance and harmony.
He also has the only correct path to spend the rest of eternity.

Bringing in the Sheaves
September 18, 1992

It is written, "He who soweth sparingly
shall reap also sparingly;
and he who soweth bountifully
shall reap also bountifully."
The times are wicked and very bad.
The saints should indeed feel quite sad.
Surely with little I rightly associate.
The role of active harvester needs be to most more inveterate.
The world almost on the edge of moral and economic survival.
Oh, how we need a revival.
By God, the Father, it must be anointed.
Yea, I wish now were the time it is appointed.
The church needs a transformation.
Therein must begin any great reformation.
It is by and by not at all holy and obedient.
In that assessment anyone could be quite confident.
Though anyone can sow a heap,
without God's will no one can reap.
In His decision all must abide.
Many pray that for a revival He would soon decide.
Oh, that salvation coming to souls would be very rife.
Only God can solve man's destruction, misery, and strife.
Oh, that newly won souls would be common as autumn's falling leaves.
Then many could rejoice at the church's bringing in the sheaves.

The Social Gospel and Other Stuff
October 25, 1992

The apostle Paul commanded Timothy to preach the Word.
He was to be diligent in season and out, it was to be heard.
He was also to reprove, rebuke, and exhort.
Paul spoke not of giving any social report.
Preaching God's Word is a full-time business.
The edification will suffer when the thrust does regress.
In strictly the gospel and wisdom you must abound.
In this you can go forever around and around.

There is an endless supply of material for such.
On doctrine, exhortation, and the Word you can't get too much.
To be Christlike is what the disciple must seek.
You can't afford to lose a single week.

In many places by the wayside the Word fell.
I hear that some preach only the social gospel.
To study and define this I can't find out.
It would waste my time, no doubt.
Why spend hours if "such and such" is in heaven
or conjuring to the millimeter the rise of the Pharisees' leaven.
Obsessions with other things is a turning away.
The shepherds have no time to don a social gospel frock.
You are not thereby tending and feeding your flock.
Would you forget to feed your child for one week?
A babe in the cradle or in Christ must have nourishment at its peak.
To the image of Christ, we are to be conforming.
Without the Word, there will be no transforming.
Upon the earth we have only a limited time to roam.
We know not when the Father shall call us home.
It is a point we need not debate.
Our rewards and eternal standing will depend upon our final state.
To spiritually grow, we must endeavor to quicken our pace.
With the sand in life's hourglass we are in a race.
Stay away from the social gospel and other stuff
or you will always be a diamond in the rough.

Seeking Enlightenment
December 6, 1992

All you who just go to and fro.
How much do you really know?
Do you just accept every matter or try
to find out the why?
Does the direction of the people and this country
suggest an impending calamity?
Consider whether you believe in God or are an atheist.
God is in control of all that does exist.
This world is not just full of evil, human gaiety, and mirth.
The glory of God does fill heaven and earth.
There is a method to all of the madness.
Satan is preying upon human lust and all does regress.
Many would ignore it and disclaim it.
It would be to you more profitable to explain it.
Surely powers on high exert their control.

Do you know or try to define your role?
Shame on you if you are only passive
and submissive.
A righteous orientated influence you should be exerting.
All that is necessary for evil to succeed is for good men to do nothing.
There are reasons for evil's increasing existence.
Most Christians are lying down and putting up no resistance.
Are you writing letters and getting into public debates?
The righteous cause is automatically lost if everyone hesitates.
You should not just be slinking down into quietude and discouragement.
You should be seeking enlightenment.
Learn and memorize God's Word to a great degree.
Learn the truth and it will make you free.
Examine your comings and goings.
There needs to be a purpose and urgency to your doings.
Time and money, you need to give.
It is not just for self we can live.
One day before God all will stand and give report.
If Christ is not living in you, you will surely fall short.

Have a Great Fall

January 10, 1993

We know Humpty dumpty sat on a wall.
He also had a terrible fall.
Many do drink from pride's cup.
Hark, you are setting yourself up.
If you get puffed up, you will surely rise.
You may one day be in for a surprise.
Some carry high class, dignity, and poise with a flair.
Your pretentious cloak of humility is as thin as the air.
Upon your present state you should surely frown.
The eventually brings all braggarts down.

Some people get facts and knowledge in their head.
Their light lava knowledge seems to thicken itself to lead.
They often think they should be the boss.
If this intermediate apprentice left, it would be no loss.
They need other people around to be the detail brains.
They then want to take the credit and get the distinctive gains.
For monetary remuneration they often get to be equal or par.
A skills evaluation would show the spread should be quite far.
To this does anyone you know fit?
Their head is so big I am surprised their pants do not split.
O Lord, I pray you bring all such people to the test

to see if they are indeed their pretended company's best.

Are any of you befuddled by such?
Cleave to and call on the Lord very much.
The Lord will help you along
even though many days' end may provoke a sad song.
To let God take control is in demand.
Put the situation into almighty God's hand.
Life may have been going along in a fretful mime.
God exalts the humble in due time.
You seem to always get the low road
while the high is the braggart's abode.
Pray, "O Lord, put this Humpty Dumpty on a high wall."
Have a great fall!

How Fares Your Libran Balance?
January 28, 1993

Not just the Libran only, a lover of justice and fairness.
In being more than just and equitable all should progress.
More need to live by the spirit of the law
rather than circumspect it by a technical flaw.
All who have a ruling position in a plant or office,
at being fair and equitable you can be no novice.
Recompense needs to be rated, evaluated,
and correctly implemented.
Solomon did ask God for wisdom to be a fair ruler
and judge the people in all that did matter.
In meting out justice he well balanced the scale.
As the wisest man he is the one most to hail.

I suggest there is another matter of importance.
Consider all God does for temporal and eternal consequence.
It was not at all a matter of human fairness to go on the cross.
In explaining the Savior's death, the human knowledge alone is at a loss.
Things are done for purposes that matter temporally
and eternally.
To say for which and how much,
can you rightly say how it is as such as such?
How do you weigh human suffering
and just exactly how is God measuring?
Consider all human and spiritual workings on the scale's one side.
Just what type of weights lie across did you decide?
The way of the cross is very difficult.
Quite contrary to human endeavors and man's result.

Even the scale's fulcrum rests on a divine finger.
Does your explanation yet progress or do you linger?
Upon the weightier things of God can you get a good grip?
I rather think you will make an empty trip.
A thesis on eternal judgement you could do in a few lines.
That is one report you can't "dress to the nines."
When it comes to God's infiniteness I plead almost total ignorance.
How fares your Libran balance?

The Most Unlikely Road
January 29, 1993

I suppose many of you have figured out your comings
and the what for of your goings.
Are your choices pretty easy to read
and you simply go ahead full speed?
How many choices do you have on the way?
I speak not of the triteness of where you drive your car each day.
A few of you know not exactly where you are going
because it is not yet in the time of the Lord's disclosing.

Some by signs are seeing the Lord will move them out
and things are strangely working, no doubt.
For some the opting of a career
is a thing very dear.
From worry one eighth grader I knew was free.
She already figured out where she would get her master's degree.
For others at the age of 24
figuring out life is still a chore.

The Lord has us often facing difficult decisions.
The Christian life has its necessary choices and revisions.
More than a task to figure out what God will do.
Guessing results often becomes a difficult cud to chew.
The experienced know one thing well and are wise
to the fact the God is full of mystery and surprise.
That God will give us the best should bring tranquility.
Most face too much with far too much anxiety.
For most I suspect the thing they nearly hate
is that many things come after a long wait.
Contemplating results is not usually a simple musing.
Evil angels are at hand playing mind games and making all confusing.
Some choices appear to be near and will occur in a snap.
Building you up too soon was an evil mental trap.
Feeding your logic and misperception they surely can.

They are 100 times wiser than any man.
They like to turn the musing of something into a mental wrangle.
An unneeded x factor striking at every angle.

So, consider only what will be.
By logic several choices you can see.
Quite logical are choices A, B, or C.
God will upstart you with a "D."
Only by mere logic and physical appearance is your mind fed.
You (unlike God) do not know what else is ahead.
You often travel ahead and can see only a "Y."
Opting the most logical you will try.
Others may later ask you of your present place or abode.
"God brought me here by taking the most unlikely road."

The Hunt
February 1, 1993

Some, I heard, sought the will of God with persistency.
They likened it to an elusive mystery.
I heard only a few words of their talk
and knew little of their walk.
A part of their purpose they did face.
There are several aspects to each individual race.

Do you have doubts about your present job and dwelling?
Some could not describe at all their present calling.
Know that a few are in a fruitless race
because God intends to move them to a new place.
To all others who have taken root
you should be bearing some kind of present fruit.
In your church you should have found a place of service.
Helping or being useful in a church is one's Christian purpose.
God did not call everyone to be an elder.
The King came to earth and was also a server.
In your proper place there are many things to be done.
Gifts to be used in edification and souls to be won.
Let not evil envelop your thinking with only fate.
Pray for peace about your present state.
Pray that in your general place and purpose that you find
from the Lord a peace of mind.
All who seek the face of God shall find his will
and know it well.
It will not be like looking for years for a needle in a haystack.
For God in all things no purpose shall lack.

Nor does God will anyone to be in a fruitless mime
or for eternal purposes to be wasting time.
To serve God you can surely completely resist.
In pursuit of worldly desires many people's time does wholly consist.
Have the pursuit of God's purpose in mind.
It is something all can surely find.

So, some abide in a place in which they will stay.
Other people are intended to move away.
God puts in them also a desire to serve.
The talents of their service is mostly in reserve.
"We are wasting our lives," is the usual debate.
Milton wrote, "They also serve who only stand and wait."

Know also for those who are "in place"
that there is a great spiritual battle amid the human race.
Your feelings of service shall digress
as Satan makes you feel really useless.
Let God's Word and power be your main resource.
You will discover that you are still on course.

You aint Got no English.
March 23, 1993

Black is hot; white is not.
Have is now: got is not.
"I got" or "Have you got?" is too common of men.
Many "aint got no" ken.
"I got" means I fetched.
Last week I got a check. If you think I still have it, you are "tetched."
"it's got" many will say.
It has got (the same) most should know is nay.
Write, wrote, has written.
Get, got, have gotten.
No auxiliaries with past tense is "fifth grade."
Contractions don't make a new correct shade.
Good grammar is something you should wish,
but most "don't got no English."
Two no's make a yes you have heard. (algebra)
To think some are double emphasizing is absurd.

I once went to a writing seminar to enhance grammatical power.
The lecturer misused "got" 16 times in one hour.
Some stress to be so fancy and high.
Your fifth or seventh grade book you should not have bid "bye."

Get your elementary book and dictionary out,
if you still have a doubt.
"You've got to have," is the real boner.
For misuse it is a real oner.
"You have gotten," you should say.
"You obtained to," makes no sense I say.
For a high school dropout, it might not be so bad.
To hear college grads today it is really sad.
Even used by the contender and the last two in the White House.
These poor euphemisms you should not espouse.
We need a "Seventh Grade Standards Act."
"The wise man loves knowledge and correction," is how you should react.
The fool comes back with a rebuff.
Do you like being "one in the rough?"

Rock-a-bye Baby
October 28, 2000

Rock-a-bye baby.
Sometimes a must and not a maybe.
Like a cool skillful monkey swinging in the treetops.
He has so much experience he should be a pops.
Like a retiree on a rocker he practiced on his swivel tilt.
He has most rhythms fine-tuned to the hilt.
Only one clue should suffice.
Have you walked around the office? (went to co-workers)
Now surely that should do.
If you do not, where were you?
Some people practice perfection to a peak.
Do you think he would drive the baby nuts with the chair's loud squeak?

(Observed of an office worker.)

Looking Ahead
June 21, 1992

A recent vacation up north was a farce.
Fishing and enjoyment were too scarce.
An undesirable vacation to spend.
Not an expected end.
Days over which to be sad.
To think of better ahead I was glad.

To all who seek God will He give an expected end.
To expectation and hope your mind must append.
Surely many days will be dreary
and of life you may become quite weary.
A few could shed many more tears
in that life has been hard for many years.
All peace and joy did circumstances perhaps rend.
Jeremiah wrote that the Lord wishes all an expected end.
For many years we were in preparation.
God has not revealed our final destination.
Life shall not be a dreary fate.
Not in vain upon God shall we await.
Yesterday and today the last role He did conceal.
Tomorrow perhaps may be the day to reveal.

A vacation was bad recently I said.
I in hope look ahead.
Another trip we shall try.
To California we will fly.
June's week was a tragedy.
July will bring a trip to the "high country."
The mountains and sea do beckon.
We will surely get there I reckon.
All need to hope in God and what is ahead.
The optimist must have this idea firmly in his head.
I write of the high country – terra incognita.
I write of the high country – mountains – terra firma.
We wait for July 21 to be the present day.
We will be heading up the San Luis Obispo way!

(the Lord finally revealed for us in June 1999
where we would go. Went to Texas for 15 years.
We were tossing for 15 years on this. In 2014
we came back to Wisconsin to retire.)

On Love
July 5, 1992

Love is like being a servant.
One can talk or make it apparent.
From some it can only be solicited by great appeal.
With others it is easily practiced and with great zeal.
Various topics on love can fill many a book.
But only at three aspects shall we take a look.

Love is a choice.
Yea, like your mouth, you decide if you activate your voice.
In a concept one can easily abide.
Doing something requires that you decide.
Many things come up as an opportunity.
Many will pass and a choice will no longer be timely.
The unsaved will always be with us.
Generally, there will always be opportunities as thus.
Many things will suddenly appear on the spot.
We must act while "the iron is yet hot."
Very quickly an opportunity will be forever lost.
We will discover later that will to us be a cost.
One must never act thinking he or she may get a reward.
It is just good and natural for people and us from the Lord.

Love is a commandment.
Not just a thing if it fits our good judgement.
We are to love the Lord our God with all our heart.
It is a concept that is to never depart.
"With all thy mind"
you will upon reading find.
This is the first and greatest commandment.
Humanly impossible to be totally obedient.

The second is to love thy neighbor
as thyself and this is more (you should concur)
than all whole
burnt offerings and sacrifices (which fully fit their role.)
These commandments can one easily speak of any day.
They are much more difficult to obey.
Think then that love is something to act upon
as well as to just meditate on.
Jesus came also as a servant.
Such a role many selfish people would lament.
Make no mistake.
Jesus' ministry is for us as well as the disciples – something in which to partake.
To wit, we have upon us a ministry.
To that we must make a choice to act upon each opportunity.

Deeds, Creeds, and Associations
July 5, 1992

It is good to do good deeds.
There are many, many needs.
We can easily see a need in almost every coming

and going.
To find something, one needs hardly meditate.
All you need do is look while you hesitate.
Oft for things people get together in a group.
Things can often be better done by an organized troop.
Herein must one exercise judgement.
Everything is not an automatic betterment.

Some groups gather only to do deeds.
While others execute them on the basis of strong creeds.
To such we need to give great discretion.
Accomplishments only must not be an overriding compassion.
All creeds must have a scriptural alignment.
At least, there can be no disagreement.
With God's values all must be in conformity.
Yea, with the Word there must be an orthodoxy.
Many do not pause
long enough to see that all is a Christly cause.

By creeds we decide upon improper or proper associations.
These must be a forefront in all relations.
Christianity you can't mimic
and work in an abortion clinic.
By providing alcohol or strong drink
you can cause a weaker brother to stumble or go over the brink.
Political discretion is lacking in many.
Examine each person's views, Christianity, and political party.
Political parties go forth as in a fight
trying to impose upon all what is right.
From what you have read and heard,
who is most likely to be obedient to God's Word?
Pick with no great flaw.
Each candidate attempts to put his thoughts into law.
To that you need to give a second thought!
Will he or she enact what by scripture you have been taught?

A common adage is that birds of a feather
flock together.
Are those in your every flock
conformed to Christ the solid rock?
Would Christ approve of all your associations' creeds?
If not, you are performing misdeeds.
Consider every group and cause you promote.
Would each one's dogma be a good thing to tote?
Decide for sure whether Christ would be proud
of your association or if you are feathering with the wrong crowd.

Highs and Lows

December 8, 1992

So many do we see.
Ponder each testimony.
Many yet a Christian novice so to try
too soon to exalt themselves so high
oft does later appall
when they do fall.
Note the apostle commended no novice to leadership
because struggling against hard things will make a bad trip.
Some known first for infamy?
Others (a few) forever purity.
Many always to be in obscurity.
Some waxing and waning in sincerity.
Some put in perspective or relative highs and relative lows.
This comparing and examining thus usually therewith goes.

Talents seem to raise some to a pedestal.
Not solid are the walls of their fortress around the citadel.
Perhaps problems run afoul the testimony
or such a great star has a rift in matrimony.
Many rue.
A victory of battle the adversary does therein do.
Bad news travels fast.
A skull and a cross bones flag is seen far when high on a mast.
A fall do all deplore.
Some we will publicly see little more.

A few lucky to be kept.
Over no sins have they wept.
Upon them evil hath not trod.
Some kept purely by the power of God.
For your good virtue take not too much credit.
Your will and God's keeping were the pair that did fit.
The why of such differentiated endings you shall not find
as you can't search God's mind.
Strive and will to purity.
Make no matter to attain fame or be in obscurity.

All to wrestle the spiritual enemy.
Keep striving to reach the high country.
Each seeing wins and defeats.
All walking different beats.
Cling always to the blood's power.
The adversary is able to bring you down any hour.
All who are pent up with pride

will take a perilous and tragic ride.
Full ahead and eyes only on the cross.
Reckon yourself fortunate to suffer no character loss.
Do not aimlessly roam
as you know not when the Savior will take you home.
One's last state will matter eternally
for good is the life ending faithfully.

For the Graduate
May 25, 1998

K through 12 were just normal years.
Henceforth the usual now disappears.
Opportunity can now be the whole world.
Where to shall my destiny now be hurled?
A wow when we think of how much to see!
Without the Lord like being alone on the biggest sea.
Destiny and purpose to realize.
Anxious for dreams to materialize.
Really wondering what shall
soon and thereafter befall.
O child of the light
in the seer's ball take no delight.
You may see a few attainments and battles being won,
but know you will not see what thereby shall be taken – one by one.
Lord, grant me a fulfilling and exciting course.
We need only be an obedient partaker from the divine source.
Over my departure be not sad.
We have more reasons to be glad.
Be joyful and give me a smile and a radiant beam.
Time has come to be off reaching for my dream.

Just Musing
May 2018

Now and then I just sit.
Perhaps to rest or to use my wit.
Never know what comes to mind.
Could be interesting I find.
Thoughts bubbling up from the spring.
This gift quite a fascinating thing.
Some or many days naught.

Like pails of water from the spring being caught.
Sometimes just sit still
and the poetic pail does fill.
Sometimes quite interesting or new.
It does surprise me too.

Chapter 8

The Gift of Poetry Examined and Dissected
(An analysis and some applications detailed)
December 3, 2020

So, you want to know how the poetic process and my mind work. We will have to take a look at how my thinking works if we can. This could be an interesting journey into my mind. Let's go!

The Gift of Poetry – A gift from God. It really has 3 parts.

1. ***It is an effervescent spring given by God***. Sometimes I just sit and concentrate and it comes forth like an endless spring. I can say it is endless because God is endless. Get the pen and paper ready when thoughts exude.

2. ***The ability to rhyme***. Rhyming is usually quite easy with this gift. I usually just write a sentence on the topic. Now the next one must rhyme. So, I write. "There I see my boyhood tree." Usually a word just pops into my head. "glee." Then often the sentence comes forth almost as fast as snapping your fingers. "Oh, how I used to climb it with such glee." Human ability on its own cannot compete with my gift from God in rhyming.

3. ***My help in rhyming***. Sometimes the rhyming word does not immediately come. Then a word is put into my head. I do not always know what it means. I must look it up in the dictionary to know how to properly use it in a sentence. This could be any of the trinity or ministering spirit. (The spiritual contest is not just one sided evil and God's angels do nothing.) One person had an image of an angel standing over me helping me with my work. The powerful addition, vocabulary, and form readily show me at times I am getting help.

The Poem *My Spring – An Intrigue* has a completely different perspective than what I just wrote above. All is true. I do indeed love to go far beyond the simplicity of things merely happening.

I do indeed ask the Lord's help in these poems. I had close to 50 foreign phrases in my one dictionary I wanted to write about. One translated "Explaining the difficult by the more difficult." I start out by meditating this phrase. Some came easily. This one went nowhere. I prayed for help. Meditated and none came. I prayed again and the same result. I went to the Lord the 3rd time and I was able to do it. This was probably the most difficult poem I ever wrote. Now I should be speaking for most of us Christians in that when we want to do something good, God is there to help us and we produce far more that a mere human effort.

Poem "For Brandon – A Prayer of Blessing."

One day in church he was sitting with his parents. I happened to look at him and the Holy Spirit said like the still small voice, "Write Brandon a prayer of blessing." That night we went home but I did not proceed yet. I was lying in bed and the voice said again, "Write Brandon a prayer of blessing." Then in a day or 2 or by the next Sunday it came the third time, "Write Brandon a prayer of blessing." O.k. Lord, I get it. Shortly thereafter I sat down to write it. As I thought about it, it came to mind he wanted to be an engineer. Then the insight and vision of the future came. God was going to greatly help him. At times an engineer must be a genius and great inventor. The Lord showed me He would help him to be so. So, after meditation of this the lines flowed out.

Poem for Cassie – A prayer of blessing. Cassie is Brandon's sister. The Lord in the same manor spoke to me to write a poem. I sat down and after some meditation the style and content just flowed out. God has in store for her great things in using abilities to glorify him.

For Christina - A prayer of blessing. One day another Christian wanted to go out for a steak at noon. We drove to the restaurant. I felt I should go back and give her my testimony. She was a Christian also. I ended up helping her and giving her some support for 7 years because her jobs were not working out and a doctor was helping her get off some meds, but went too fast. This was just a sincere prayer for some else, so just picture me or someone on their knees pleading for her. No future was shown, so just and ordinary prayer in some ways. When I gave her money I told her she was "flush," a term we used up north. Wrote "Not quite a royal flush." A double meaning- a play on words. "Isn't it Nice" tells of some of the things she did with the money.

"Oh, Galveston Island" is a special one. We were down for a day or 2 in 2013 to stay. In August I was compelled to go back for a visit. Strong urge within me. I liked the place and this was my favorite place in Texas to visit. So late August or early September we were there for a night or two. We took the city tour on the wheeled duck boat. Near the end the tour guide said, "We are due for a hurricane, we have not had one in 5 years." A strong "no" came into my head, not in the next 10 years either. I kept praying, "Lord, if this be of you let it grow stronger or take it away." It became stronger and stronger. So later as I sat down to write it became obvious in God show me the why of it as He wanted to show the place, "Grace, mercy, and restoration." You will see that in the poem and see the neat ending I have. So now only 3 years to go.

"My Odyssey." I thought of the Superman movie of when Clark became an adult. One of the crystals revealed to him that his father wanted to take him through the galaxy on a ten year learning adventure. Then it came into my mind that the Lord was going to take me on a life time odyssey, of which many things would be written in my poems. Not only would there be new knowledge, but the forms of the poems would be new and interesting to me. Example – The Grams – I write a message down the left side of the page., then write a poem using those letters. Just go through my table of contents – each book has one – Things like "Death and the Afterlife,", "Wisdom and Insight," "Back to the Future," "The Great Fall." The great fall is explained in book 2 and you get to see both poems. These 2 start out the book. You get to see the table of contents and the first 3 poems in it or so.

The Grams – I write a message down the left side of the page, then the sentence starts with that letter. Neat structure. See, the odyssey continues!

www.ingramcontent.com/pod-product-compliance
Lightning Source LLC
Chambersburg PA
CBHW081700120626
46550CB00010B/2964